STAN SMITH:

SOME PEOPLE THINK I'M A SHOE!

SOME PEOPLE THINK

STAN SMITH:

Edited by Stan Smith

with Richard Evans

I'M A SHOE!

Rizzoli
NEW YORK

New York · Paris · London · Milan

To all the people around the world who wear Stan Smiths.

– Stan Smith, 2018

TABLE OF CONTENTS

Foreword   8
By Pharrell Williams

Stan Smith: The Man   12
By Stan Smith

Stan Smith: The Shoe   34
By Gary Aspden

Stan Smith: A to Z   49

Stan Smith: 15 Stories   298
Portraits by Juergen Teller

Acknowledgments   331

Credits   332

FOREWORD

BY PHARRELL

It gives me so much pleasure to write a few words about a man and a company that have entered my life over the past few years and have come to mean so much to me.

A man and his shoe—but no ordinary man and no ordinary shoe. Reaching past fifty years, the pair of them have written new meaning into a sporting partnership, spreading their wings to embrace the world of fashion and leisure.

Long before I met Stan Smith, I had, of course, seen the shoe. As a kid growing up in Virginia Beach, I noticed people wearing them. Then, so much later when I had joined adidas and realized that the Stan Smith shoe was such a vital part of what the company had to offer, I finally got to meet the man himself at the U.S. Open. In five minutes we had a rapport—because of the man he is. In five minutes I knew it was OK, everything was cool.

The fact that we looked different and came from different backgrounds had no bearing on anything. For decades his shoe has spoken to people from all walks of life living in every nation on earth. Just like the man himself. It was really interesting that I felt so comfortable in his world, in this man's company.

I am not a tennis player, and as we watched the matches, I needed to learn about the tennis scoring system and found no problem in asking him questions that might have sounded simplistic. Stan does more than answer. He educates you in a manner that leaves you feeling totally comfortable as you soak up the information.

As I got to know him, it became clear to me that Stan has always been this same calm, patient person. You see it when you meet his family, when you watch him teach kids at his tennis camp, or when he moves with grace and ease through rooms crowded with important, and sometimes self-important, people.

It is then that the shoe steps into play its part because it acts as the common denominator. Everyone wears it, sometimes on unlikely occasions. Because it is elegant, because it speaks to fashion, because it has created fashion.

And music. Because for me, as an artist, there is no fashion without music and no music without fashion. Like a great song that has survived the ages, the Stan Smith shoe has undergone slight variations, but the melody has stayed the same. There is never any need to tamper with class.

Stan Smith, of course, exudes class, which remains the underlying factor of his partnership with a fashion item that is totally democratic. No two people, when they wear the shoe, seem alike. It's a shoe for the individual, complementing different people in its own unique way. And it is unique. It's a rare thing to have produced something of this quality and longevity and adidas knows it. When I visit the company headquarters in Paris, I notice how often Stan's name comes up and the respect with which it is spoken. That's because of the man—and the product of which they can be justly proud.

The Stan Smith shoe has become a living icon and you will find out how it became so in the pages that follow. It is quite a story.

PHARRELL WILLIAMS   PHARRELL WILLIAMS

STAN SMITH: THE MAN

One of the few disappointments in my tennis career were my big size 13 feet—yet the shoe I eventually wrapped around them enabled me to become better known than I could have ever envisaged.

By Stan Smith

THE MAN THE MAN

Stan Smith, Boston, 1961.
"Obviously I did not have
a shoe contract." – S.S.

THE MAN THE MAN

Growing up in my birthplace of Pasadena, California where my father was a tennis coach, I did not take to tennis immediately—basketball was my game as a young child—but, by fifteen, I had started to play it seriously and had become a fan. So I eagerly volunteered for ball boy duties at the Los Angeles Tennis Club when they were about to stage a Davis Cup tie between the United States and Mexico. I had turned sixteen and, being tall, I had arrived at that gangly stage of adolescence that is so often a difficult period in any kid's life. There were a group of us being tested for mobility, agility and ball sense. Everything at the LATC happened under the eagle eye of Perry T. Jones, a rigid, self-opinionated disciplinarian who ruled over southern Californian tennis at the time.

After the tests were completed I discovered I had not been chosen. I was, apparently, too awkward and clumsy. I was mortified! Maybe if I had been wearing adidas sneakers? Well, no, that was not the problem. It was me. I had to get my feet sorted out and work on my mobility. So I started jumping rope for about ten minutes every day and tried to ignore the fact that the other players used to laugh at me. It paid off.

Maybe I never became the fastest player ever to set foot on a tennis court but long strides, a big reach at the net and a tall, strong frame enabled me to base my game on power and, to everyone's surprise including

Top: At the US National Championships, 1963. *Bottom:* Holding one of my first winner's trophies, 1962. *Opposite*: My parents, Ken and Rhoda Smith.

my own, I won a sanctioned tournament at Santa Barbara. Lou and Linda Crosby, two great tennis enthusiasts who ran the Pasadena Tennis Patrons, were thrilled. They had helped me enormously, as had Pancho Segura, the little pigeon-toed Ecuadorian who had over-come the considerable disadvantage of being born with rickets to become a star on the Jack Kramer professional tour.

Segura, a wise-cracking jokester who was only really serious when analyzing a tennis match, used to come over to Pasadena High School on Saturdays to coach me on our peach-colored courts. The unusual setting was a perfect fit for Segura who was unlike anyone else I have ever known. Just being around him was an education in more ways than one. Most of his jokes were unprintable but you were never bored! We worked together whenever we could. Mostly at the Pasadena High School or the Beverly Hills Tennis Club but he was always popping up in my career at opportune moments. Many years later, when I was making the long trek from the clubhouse to the stadium at the West Side Tennis Club in Forest Hills to play Jan Kodes in the final of the U.S. Open, he fell in step and told me exactly what I needed to know.

"You gotta do three things: 1. Serve kickers to his forehand; he can't control them. 2. Got to lob him after first shot. 3. Run around to your forehand off his

Top: Bob Lutz and me at the LA Tennis Club for the Southern California Junior Championships, 1964. *Bottom:* At a clinic for intercity kids in Washington DC, during my time in the Army, 1971.

My junior days pre-moustache and
pre-adidas, 1964.

THE   MAN   THE   MAN

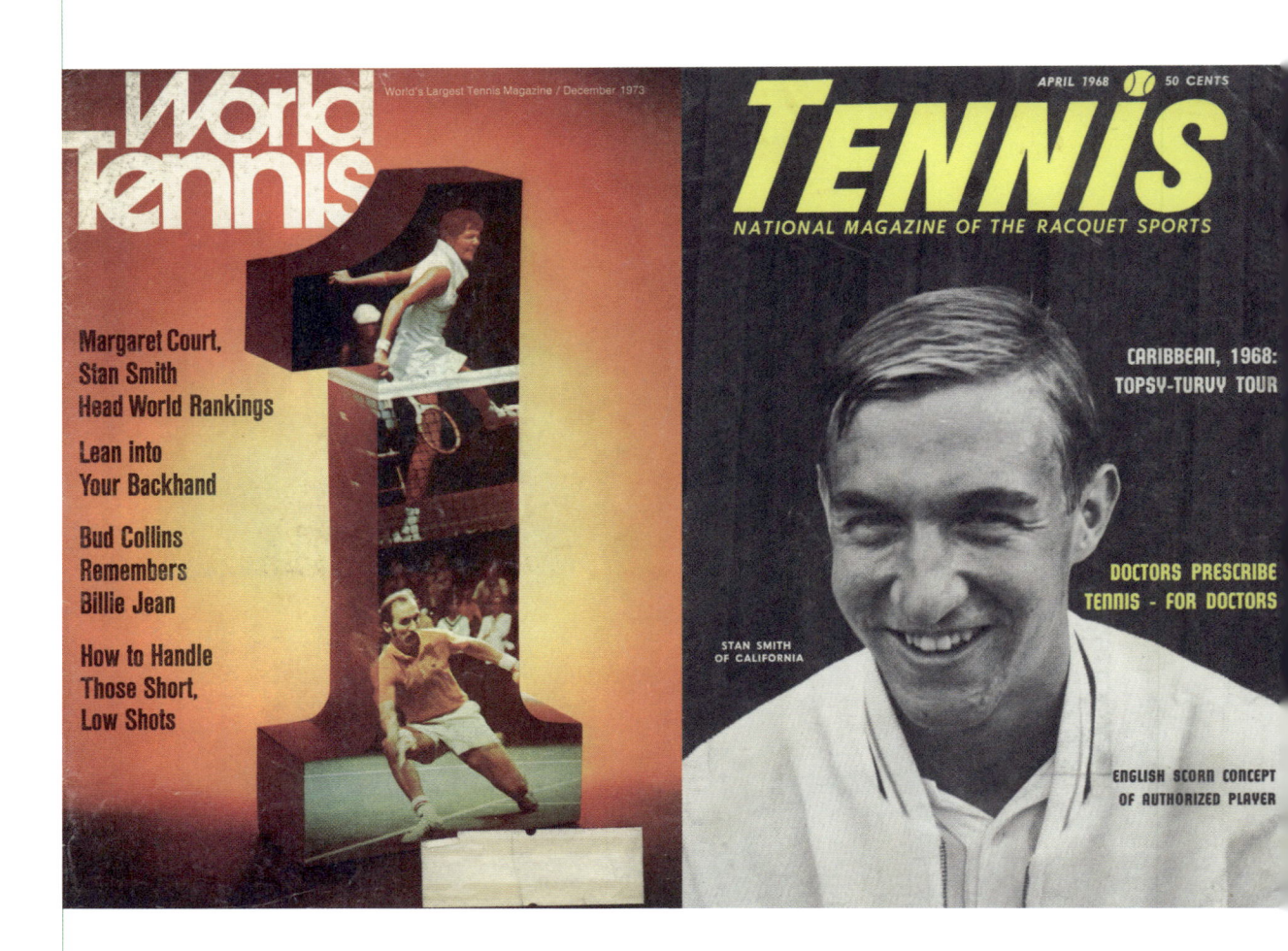

THE   MAN   THE   MAN

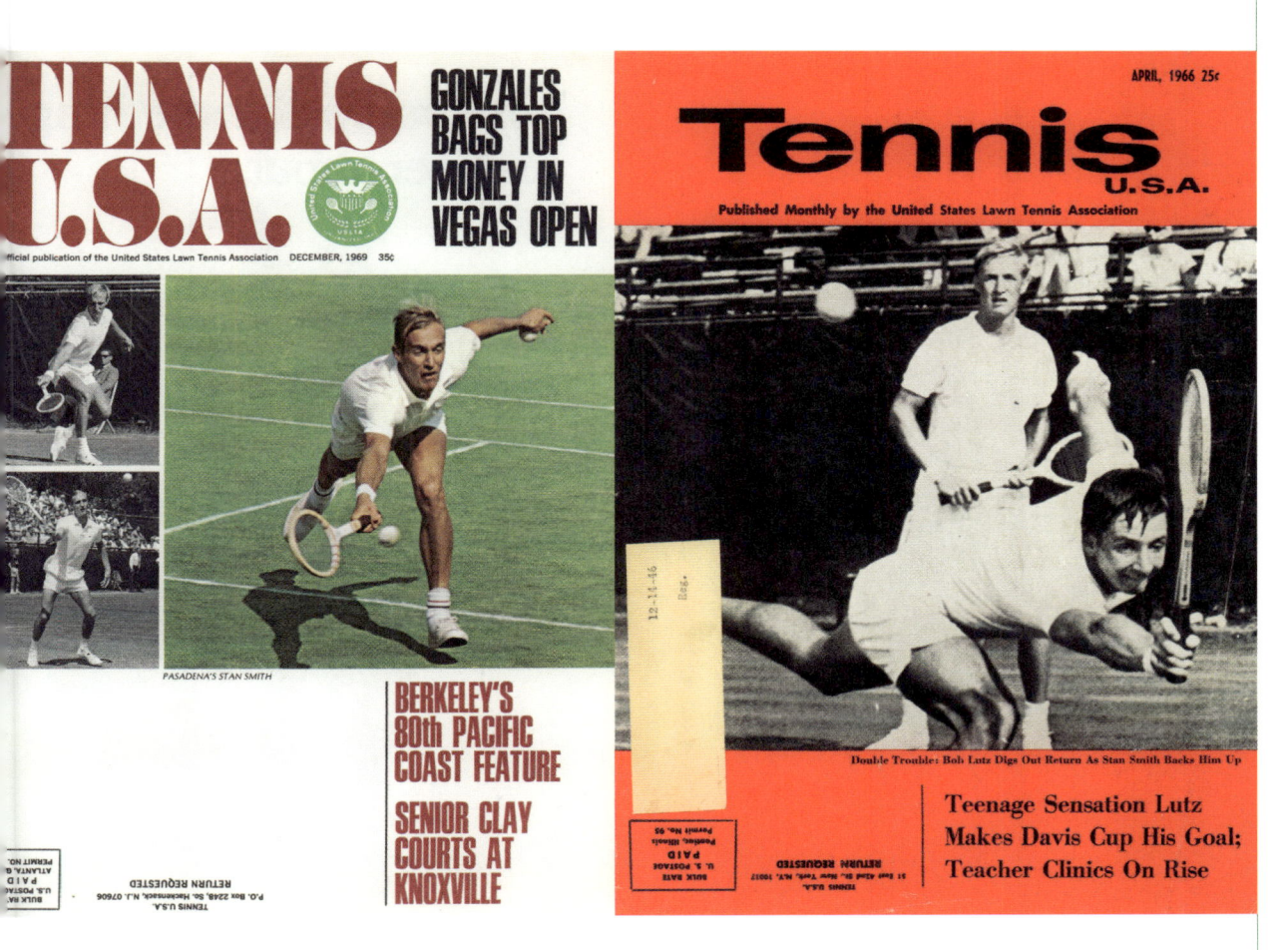

Various magazine covers that I kept from over the years.

19

THE   MAN   THE   MAN

second serve." I listened. And, following Pancho's advice, I won my first Grand Slam singles title, having already won the U.S. Open doubles with my career-long partner, Bob Lutz, in 1968. Looking back at having won the U.S. National Junior title in Kalamazoo, Michigan, early in my career, I knew dropping basketball to concentrate on tennis had been the right move. I went on to play four years on the tennis team at USC, and it wasn't long before I was able to step up to the main tour. The world was opening up and I started seeing a lot of it. In London, playing the winter indoor tournament at Wembley, I reached match point against the fearsome Pancho Gonzalez but lost. I needed a kind word after that and I was lucky that the great Jack Kramer was there to provide it. "Don't worry, kid!" he said, "You're playing well. Bit unlucky there."

Remarks like that from the right person have a big impact and I received another confidence boost when in 1970 I qualified for the first-ever Masters tournament, in Tokyo. I heard Ken Rosewall, already a legend in the game for his skill and longevity, saying in an interview that he considered me one of the favorites for the title. That gave me a big boost and I went out and proved him right by beating him in the six-man round robin format. That win clinched the title for me during a week that saw ten thousand Japanese singing "Happy Birthday" on my twenty-fourth birthday before my match—a somewhat unique experience!

Less gratifying was the cable I received from the U.S. Army: "Report to the Induction Center in Los Angeles by December 16th," it read. That was the next day! But the time change which enables you to gain a day flying East, saved me, and Private Smith reported for two years in the military on time. I was also $15,000 richer, allowing me to forego some Army pay and take excess leave so as to spend Christmas at home with the family. I played a lot of tennis in the Army and was given special dispensation to represent the United States in the Davis Cup. To play for my country had always been number one on my list of four things I set out to do as a tennis player. The others were to become No. 1 in the

Reaching No. 1 in the US for the first time, 1970. *Opposite:* Receiving flowers on my 24th birthday, just before the deciding match in the first Masters tournament in Tokyo, 1970.

U.S., which I achieved for the first time in 1969; to win Wimbledon, which I did in 1972; and to become No. 1 in the world which was achieved in 1971 and '72, just before the advent of the ATP computer ranking. Being chosen for the Davis Cup team that was due to play the British West Indies, in Richmond, Virginia, alongside Arthur Ashe, Charlie Pasarell, Clark Graebner and Bob Lutz, was a huge stepping stone to achieving my other goals.

In 1971 my agent and good friend Donald Dell had just relinquished the Davis Cup captaincy after a short but successful tenure and he had, by then, become very much part of my life. Donald was always making deals and none turned out to be more successful than the one he had made on my behalf the following year with adidas.

Donald had already established a strong relationship with another go-getter, Horst Dassler, who was head of the burgeoning clothing company. I knew something was brewing when Dell came up to me at the French Open in 1971 and said, "We have a meeting with Horst at 10:30." "I can't make that, Donald," I replied. "I have a match at 12:00!" "Not 10:30 a.m.," was the reply. "Tonight at 10:30 p.m.!" The timing was appropriate, because this nocturnal meeting was at a Parisian night club just off the boulevard Montparnasse called Elle et Luis. The name became more apparent when, on arrival, you were seated by waiters who were dressed up as men but were actually women. Cross-dressing was the theme at this cabaret as well and it was against this unorthodox backdrop that I first spoke to adidas about wearing their shoe.

Horst Dassler was anxious to expand his shoe market beyond France, especially to the United States. But it was a little delicate because their shoe at the time carried the name of Robert Haillet, a very popular former French No. 1 who had played on the Kramer tour. Horst suggested that I start wearing the Haillet shoe while they initiated a slow change. Robert's name would remain on the heel while mine would be on the side. Later my photo was added onto the tongue. After a couple of years, Haillet's name was dropped.

I reached the final of Wimbledon in 1972 but had to remain patient. Saturday's play was rained off and so, for the first

In Africa with Arthur Ashe, State Department tour, 1971. *Opposite:* Horst Dassler with portrait of his father and adidas founder, Adi Dassler, 1985.

THE MAN　　　　　　　　　　　　　　　　　　　　　　　　THE MAN

THE　　MAN　　　　　　　　　　　　　　　THE　　MAN

THE   MAN   THE   MAN

adidas Stan Smith Haillet, 1973.

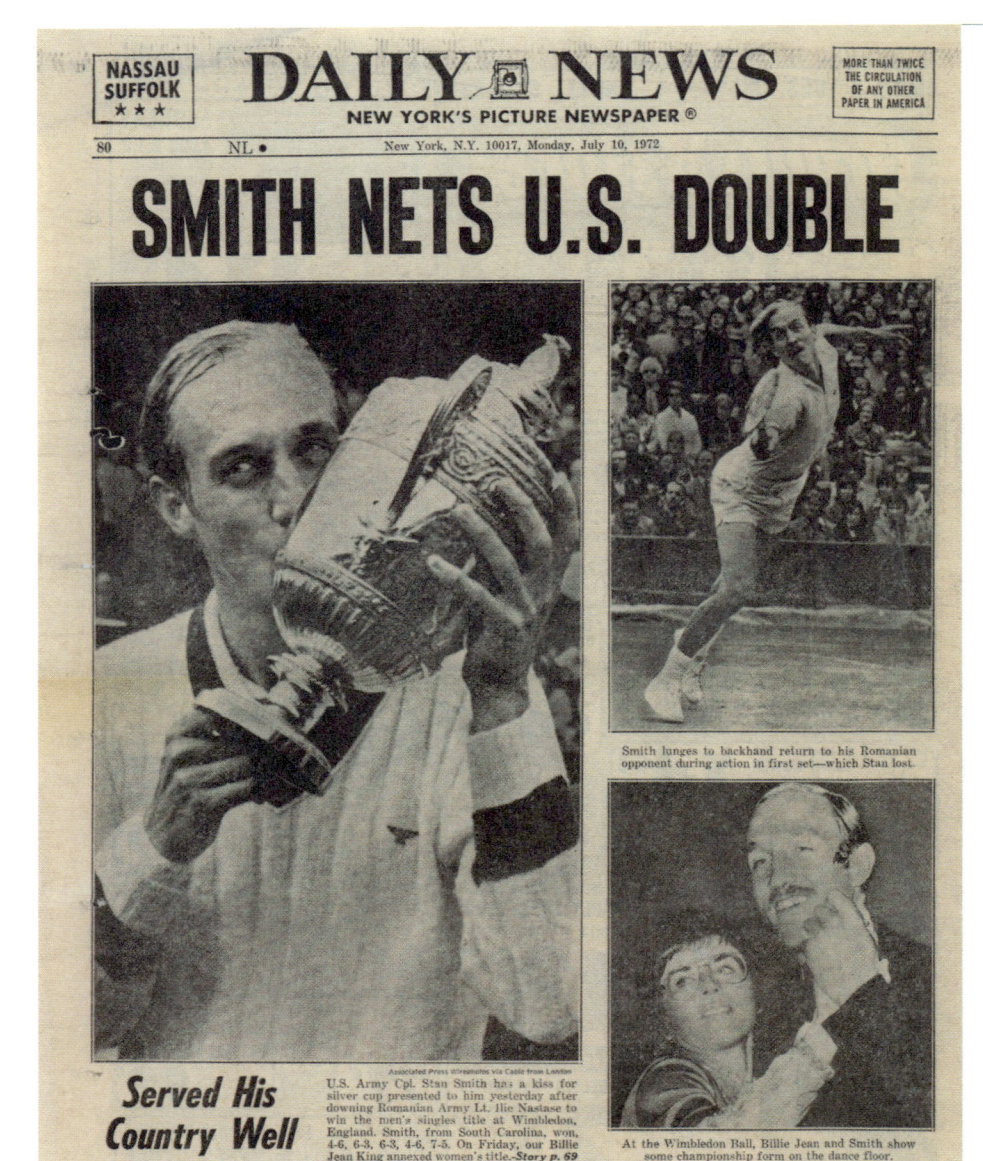

THE MAN THE MAN

DAILY NEWS
NEW YORK'S PICTURE NEWSPAPER

New York, N.Y. 10017, Monday, July 10, 1972

SMITH NETS U.S. DOUBLE

Served His Country Well

U.S. Army Cpl. Stan Smith has a kiss for silver cup presented to him yesterday after downing Romanian Army Lt. Ilie Nastase to win the men's singles title at Wimbledon, England. Smith, from South Carolina, won, 4-6, 6-3, 6-3, 4-6, 7-5. On Friday, our Billie Jean King annexed women's title. —*Story p. 69*

Smith lunges to backhand return to his Romanian opponent during action in first set—which Stan lost.

At the Wimbledon Ball, Billie Jean and Smith show some championship form on the dance floor.

time a Wimbledon final was played on a Sunday. Until then organized sport on Sundays was not allowed in Britain but times were changing.

Ilie Nastase, the mercurially talented Romanian who was also an adidas player, was my opponent and I knew it wasn't going to be easy. We had played several times before, often in Davis Cup and I had won most of them so I knew what to expect. We called him "Nasty," which he could be, despite his basically warm and generous nature. I knew keeping my concentration would be the key. He was wound up so tight that tantrums were inevitable and he complained frequently and loudly to his agent in the stands about his string tension which the poor man could do nothing about. The interruptions ruined the flow and rhythm of the match but, eventually, I reached two match points on his serve at 5—4 in the fifth set. He escaped from those and I eventually managed to close it out 7—5. I was thrilled, there is no greater title in tennis than Wimbledon champion but, after a while, a reaction set in which, I think, hits a lot of people who have striven mightily to attain a goal. "Is that all there is?" I asked myself.

Top: Ilie Nastase, 1972. *Bottom:* Waiting for the rain to stop to play the Wimbledon final, 1972. *Opposite:* Making headlines, 1972.

THE   MAN

Happily, the answer was "no." I enjoyed my best year in 1973, winning seven out of eleven tournaments on the WCT tour, beating Rod Laver on four consecutive occasions as we travelled through cities like St. Louis, Munich, Brussels, and Atlanta, and then got the better of Arthur Ashe in the WCT Dallas final. I kept on going, in retrospect playing too much in the process, and by 1975 my elbow started to become a problem. I had surgery on it in 1977 and managed to partner with Lutz to a fifth Grand Slam doubles title at the U.S. Open in 1980. But, four years later, at the age of thirty-eight, I knew it was time to call it quits.

I was lucky to get invited to commentate for NBC at Wimbledon and other tournaments almost immediately, and working with great producers and people in the commentating business like Bud Collins and Dick Enberg for the next five years eased the transition. After a while, I found myself on the senior tour and participating in charity fundraisers. In 1986, the USTA asked me to be the Director of Coaching for their newly formed Player Development program. I found great satisfaction in my new role of teaching instead of playing. I have been the Touring Pro at Sea Pines Resort on Hilton Head Island for the last forty-seven years. This property was the brainchild of Charles Fraser in the 1960s and I fell in love with it when I visited in 1971. Over the years, the Sea Pines tennis facility

Top: Interviewing Mary Carillo at the Du Pont All American tournament, Hilton Head, SC, 1988. *Bottom:* Bill Murray, Ahmad Rashad, and me at the Duke Children's Classic charity event in the early 1980s.

"Even for kids it's important to warm up and work on flexibility before actually hitting balls." – S.S.

THE   MAN   THE   MAN

Come Play Where The Champions Play

This former US Open and Wimbledon champion is as at home on the course as he is on the court. Sea Pines Touring Pro, Stan Smith is an accomplished golfer who enjoys the beauty and challenge of the famed Harbour Town Golf Links. Site of the MCI Heritage Classic and the 1989 Nabisco Championships, Harbour Town is a favorite of PGA TOUR professionals. The dramatic Ocean and Sea Marsh courses are two of the best surprises on Hilton Head and our PGA teaching professionals offer an array of clinics, lesson and exhibitions, year-round.

Under the guidance of Stan Smith, tennis at Sea Pines has flourished. Home to the nationally televised Family Circle Magazine Cup, the 29-court Sea Pines Racquet Club at Harbour Town has set the standard for tennis programs across America. You can sharpen your game with private lessons, innovative clinics and instructional programs for all skill levels.

So come play where the champions play... play Sea Pines!

Sea Pines
PLANTATION
P.O. Box 7000
Hilton Head Island, SC 29938
803-785-3333 or 1-800-845-6131

For more information, call...
Harbour Town Golf Links 803-671-2446 • Ocean & Sea Marsh 803-671-2436
Sea Pines Racquet Club 803-671-2494

grew from 8 to 30 courts and hosted many nationally televised events. For twenty-five years, the Family Circle Cup tournament was the most televised women's-only event in the world. Over the years I have been fortunate enough to see a great many resorts around the world and I truly believe that none can beat what Sea Pines Resort offers to visitors and residents. It has been a wonderful place to raise our family as well.

In 2002, Billy Stearns and I formed the Smith Stearns Tennis Academy at Sea Pines Resort for junior players with hopes of playing college or professional tennis. BJ Stearns now is the Director and we have about 50 students training year-round on the courts, in the gym, and at tournaments. As a mentor and coach, it has been a real pleasure to help these committed young players develop both on and off the court.

Margie and I support many charities on Hilton Head. We feel it is important to give back to the community. These include the Heritage Classic Foundation, Hilton Head Heroes, Volunteers in Medicine, and the Boys & Girls Club. The Heritage Classic Foundation was formed to run the professional Golf Tournament and provide assistance to many charities in South Carolina Lowcountry. Hilton Head Heroes brings families with young children suffering from life-threatening illnesses to Hilton Head Island for a resort vacation. Volunteers in Medicine recruits retired doctors who freely offer their services to people who cannot afford health care. Margie and I have been committed to the Boys & Girls since 1996. I became the Chairman of the Capital Campaign to build a permanent clubhouse and now I serve on the Board of Trustees. Margie is a committed volunteer working as an academic tutor. It's such fun, as well as such a privilege, to be able to help and watch them grow.

My family decked out in adidas clothing and my shoes, 1989. *Opposite:* Standing on the 18th green at Sea Pines, with the famous lighthouse in the background, 1982.

THE   MAN   THE   MAN

Smith family portrait, 2016.

"I never dreamed that all my children would wear Stan Smiths, let alone my grandchildren!" – S.S.

STAN SMITH: THE SHOE

When discussing athletic footwear I am often asked "What is the greatest trainer of all time?" My immediate answer is invariably the "Stan Smith."

By Gary Aspden

When discussing athletic footwear I am often asked, "What is the greatest sneaker of all time?" My immediate answer is invariably the "Stan Smith."

Over the years I have built up a fairly extensive collection of vintage adidas shoes, so asking me what my personal favorites are is like asking a music fan for their all-time favorite track—it can change depending on what day you ask me on but choosing "the greatest" shoe has to go beyond the fickleness of my own taste. Putting my ever-changing personal selections aside, there is no question that in the world of sneakers the shoe that we know nowadays as the Stan Smith is in a league all its own.

Opposite: adidas catalog, 1969/70.

THE SHOE THE SHOE

115030 "Haillet"
A top class leather tennis shoe worn by the world's best tennis players. Extremely light and comfortable soft white leather uppers form instantly to the shape of the foot.

Elegant styling with lace-to-toe derby cut (1), SOFT-PROTECT foam padding surrounds ankles (2) heel and achilles tendon (3). adidas has developed an extremely longwearing shell sole (4) with an unusual non-skidding design (5). Hundreds of tiny rubber nobs provide excellent footing on all types of tennis surfaces. Adjustable adidas arch support (6), elastic nylon heel counter (7). Look for the distinctive adidas heel patch (8) as your sure sign of quality.

USA DAVIS CUP TEAM
L-R Stan Smith, Donald Dell, Arthur Ashe, Bob Lutz.

THE   SHOE   THE   SHOE

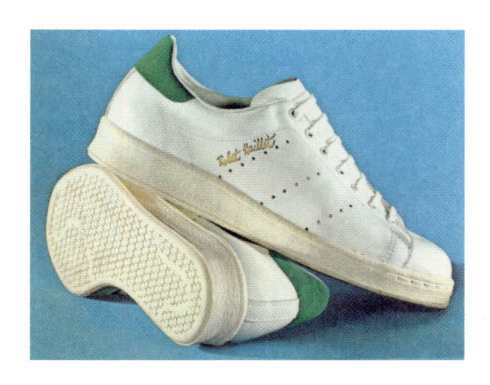

There have been innumerable iterations of this shoe spanning fifty years that are all based on a template that was established in the mid 1960s with the first all-leather tennis shoe called the adidas Haillet. The shoe was created in white leather to meet the strict white regulations of the courts, but what personified these shoes was the substitution of the iconic Three Stripes for three lines of vented air holes to better ventilate the shoe. These vent holes were seen as a technological advancement at the time, but the by-product of this was that it gave a clean, modernist aesthetic to the shoe. The open eyestay and minimal branding on the tongue and heel further differentiated them from other adidas tennis styles of this era, like the adidas Newcombe. These shoes laid the foundations for an often-imitated classic piece of product design whose enduring mass appeal is testament to the quality of its design.

It all began with the adidas Haillet, which was the signature shoe of the French tennis player Robert Haillet (who was involved in the design of the original shoe) that became the footwear of choice for rising tennis star Stan Smith a few years later. As Stan's popularity and success on the court grew he became the shoe's new endorsee. The Haillet shoes he played in were produced in a co-branded version as the Haillet Smith for a few years until eventually the shoe was produced solely under Stan's name as the adidas Stan Smith in 1978. A portrait of a clean-shaven Stan was added to the tongue, although this iconic image was not the truest representation of the man, as this portrait was done during the only six months of his adult life when he was without a moustache!

While the shoes' popularity on the courts of the 1970s was indisputable, a new phenomenon was beginning to hatch for them in a very different arena at that time. David Bowie appeared in press shots around 1977 wearing a cream shirt, tie, chinos, and Stan Smiths (without socks). Given Bowie's huge influence as a fashion icon as well as a musician, wearing a pair of tennis shoes with this outfit was a massive statement.

adidas catalog, 1969/70. *Opposite*:
David Bowie by Snowdon, 1976.

Around that time his influence was immeasurable; he had already inspired a whole new style of dress for working-class, British soccer-following youths with his look in the opening scene of Nic Roeg's film *The Man Who Fell to Earth*—an image that was also used on the cover of his Low album. His long fringe, duffel coat, parallel trousers, and footwear were emulated to set a new fashion agenda that planted the seeds for a style tribe who were given labels like "Scallies" and "Perry Boys" and later became generically known as "soccer casuals." Coincidentally, around 1978 these floppy fringed, Bowie-loving youths, who had already been wearing three-stripe soccer training shoes like the Samba, picked up on the Stan Smith as the new essential and their staple footwear of choice. This very British movement wasn't well documented at the time and passed under the radar of the newspapers and magazines of the day, however, author Kevin Sampson was the person who first brought this unknown youth cult into the media through his letters to *The Face* magazine. Kevin later authored the fictional book *Awaydays*, inspired by his experiences growing up in Merseyside, England, during this period. The book was later made into a cult film of the same name where the lead character Carty is featured throughout wearing the Stan Smith. John Lennon was another descendant of Merseyside who gravitated towards the shoe. He famously wore adidas sneakers in Abbey Road studios during the recording of "Strawberry Fields"—a radical footwear choice at the time—and as his musical career progressed through the 1970s he was often seen in Stan Smiths.

While the adidas Superstar may have played a leading role in the look of early hip-hoppers, with its shell toe and basketball roots, the Stan Smith was one of its understated costars. They were picked up by a number of early hip-hop pioneers and in 1986, around the time of their seminal album *License to Ill*, they were the shoe of choice for MCA of the Beastie Boys. Hip-hop was always about aspiration, so it was inevitable that the rappers were going to buy into the sophistication and affluence associated with the Stan Smith. In his album *The Blueprint*, Jay-Z mentioned the shoe:

adidas France Tennis product catalog, 1980. *Opposite:* Yoko Ono and John Lennon, 1980.

THE SHOE THE SHOE

THE SHOE   THE SHOE

> "Lampin' in the Hamptons
> The weekends man, the Stan Smith adidas and the Campus
> Or playin' guts on the cruise,
> Hermès boat shoes
> The Izod bucket on,
> I'm so old school."
>
> – Jay-Z

On one of the occasions that I have had the pleasure of meeting Stan he mentioned how pleased he was about Jay's lyric. Despite the fact that he is a sporting icon whose face and name have been associated with a shoe that had sold tens of millions of pairs worldwide, he was flattered to have finally achieved a level of "street credibility" with his beloved grandchildren through a namecheck from a rapper!

The shoes have maintained an ongoing appeal among musicians, with artists like Bernard Sumner of New Order, Shaun Ryder of the Happy Mondays, Mike Skinner of The Streets, and Damon Albarn of Gorillaz regularly adopting them.

adidas Tennis catalog, 1996. *Opposite:* adidas Originals x Stonewall Stan Smith "Pride" Pack, 2016.

In the 1990s Stan Smiths had become standard issue for French B-boys in the suburbs of Paris . . . In fact the shoe had become standard issue for almost *everyone* in Paris (and the rest of France, for that matter). In the mid '90s the Stan Smith was not ranged here in the U.K., so British Stan fans would be forced to acquire pairs on trips to the French capital, where they were constantly available in the adidas range. In preparation for their 2014 relaunch there was a public uproar in France with online petitions aimed at adidas when the Stan Smith was taken out of the French market to reposition its level of distribution.

To add to the shoe's aspirational value the fashion pack began to pick up on the shoes in the '90s. They began to become the footwear of choice for backstage supermodels, and in 1993 in style bible *The Face*, Naomi Campbell was shot nude by Ellen Von Unwerth wearing a custom pair of Stans that were spray-painted in silver. Years later Kate Moss even lent her name and face to a limited run of Stan Smiths to support the Platform Six exhibition in London (a charity exhibition that raised money for the LGBT+ charity Stonewall). Platform Six also saw artists like the late Judy Blame and the Chapman Brothers along with the likes of Kylie Minogue and Elton John creating one-off custom versions of the shoe for auction. There were many more crossovers with the world of high fashion with

with Marc Jacobs frequently wearing the shoe as well as the likes of Rei Kawakubo from Comme des Garçons adopting it as a staple in her everyday wardrobe. When Phoebe Philo began wearing them during her reign at Celine, it was like the fashion appeal of this design classic for women was reignited all over again.

Throughout the 1990s most classic adidas styles were "buffed up" with additional padding in their construction, and the Stan Smith was no exception. This period saw the Stan Smith 2 featuring its extra padded tongue and linear adidas logo patch (with "Stan Smith" in text underneath) overtaking its predecessor as the most popular version of the shoe globally. There was also a moment around 1997 where the Stan Smith Comfort, with its Velcro fastenings, became a must-have, ultra-hip shoe. The popularity of this "Stans on steroids" phase lasted over a decade before the eventual return to a more pared-down version of the shoe with that familiar printed portrait a decade or so later. In spite of this global trend, Japan—with its audience of product purists—was interestingly the only country at the time that continued to range the undiluted Stan Smith 1s season in, season out. These were available as a constant in Tokyo in a basic white with the green, red, or navy-blue sign-off alongside versions with white soles and colored uppers of all red, all black, and

adidas Stan Smith "Comfort", 2018.
Opposite: adidas France Tennis product catalog, 1980.

all blue. This seems relatively naïve now, but at the time it was seen as an extensive offering before adidas Originals became a full-fledged division of the adidas company, resulting in the shoe seeing innumerable color and material iterations since then. Back in 2002 adidas even released a high-top version of the Stan Smith followed a few years later by the Sleek version aimed at the women's market. While the core white shoe remains ever popular, the base foundations of the Stan Smith itself have continued to evolve with the new developments in footwear creation. In recent years we have seen versions that adopted the latest Primeknit technology to give the shoe a knitted upper.

Over the decades the aesthetic of the shoe has arguably "influenced" the design of a host of other footwear silhouettes from brands outside of adidas (some would say copied!) as well as sending waves of influence through the design of other footwear inside adidas. From the adidas Master to the referee shoe, the adidas Official, and a host of styles in between, that basic vent-holed aesthetic continues to permeate right through to today with hybrid Originals shoes like the adidas Lacombe. The reach of the Stan's influence even extended into the inclusion of a Stan derivative shoe in Japan's adidas Safety range—sneakers that were produced under license for Japanese workmen back in the 1990s with reinforced steel-toe caps!

Top: adidas Stan Smith Primeknit, Heel, 2014. *Bottom:* adidas Lacombe SPZL, 2017. *Opposite* adidas Shoe Chart, 1978.

TENNIS

3287 Forest Hills

3281 Tennis Special

AF 1121 ATP Outdoor

AF 1846 ATP Indoor

3262 Tom Okker Prof.

AF 1080 Nastase Master

AF 1729 Nastase

AF 1028 Stan Smith

THE SHOE

The twenty-first century saw the rise of adidas's collaborations with streetwear and high fashion and the Stan Smith was a key catalyst within a number of them. The shoe has featured within third-party collaborations with a host of partners and brands, such as Neighborhood, 84 Lab, Colette, Mastermind, Club 75, 10 Deep, and White Mountaineering. The Stan Smith was seized upon by Billionaire Boy's Club founder Pharrell Williams, who customized pairs with his own handwriting and doodling for the shoes he would wear in public appearances. He went on to create a quantity of these one-of-a-kind Stan Smiths that were auctioned for his charity through Parisian retailer Colette, as well as various interpretations for his adidas Originals range. When Raf Simons collaborated with adidas on the Stan Smith it appears that he understood that good design isn't necessarily about what is added, but is often about what isn't added. On his version he made simple tweaks to the shoe, offsetting his own portrait against Stan's and reworking the vent holes into an "R." Raf's interpretation of the Stan Smith gave the underlying message that the original couldn't be bettered. It felt like in spite of all his power and influence with fashion and culture, Raf knew there was little that could be done to improve on the simplicity of this tennis shoe—a shoe that is now considered a masterpiece of product design and a cultural icon.

Custom hand-painted adidas Stan Smith by Pharrell Williams exclusive for Colette, 2014.

THE SHOE THE SHOE

ADIDAS ORIGINALS　　　　　　　　　　　　　ŌBYO　X　KAZUKI　X　JAM

48

ADIDAS ORIGINALS　　　　　　　　　　　　　ŌBYO　X　KAZUKI　X　JAM

STAN　　SMITH　　"WHITE"　　　　　　　　　　　　　　　　　　　　　　　　　　　　　　　　　　　2011

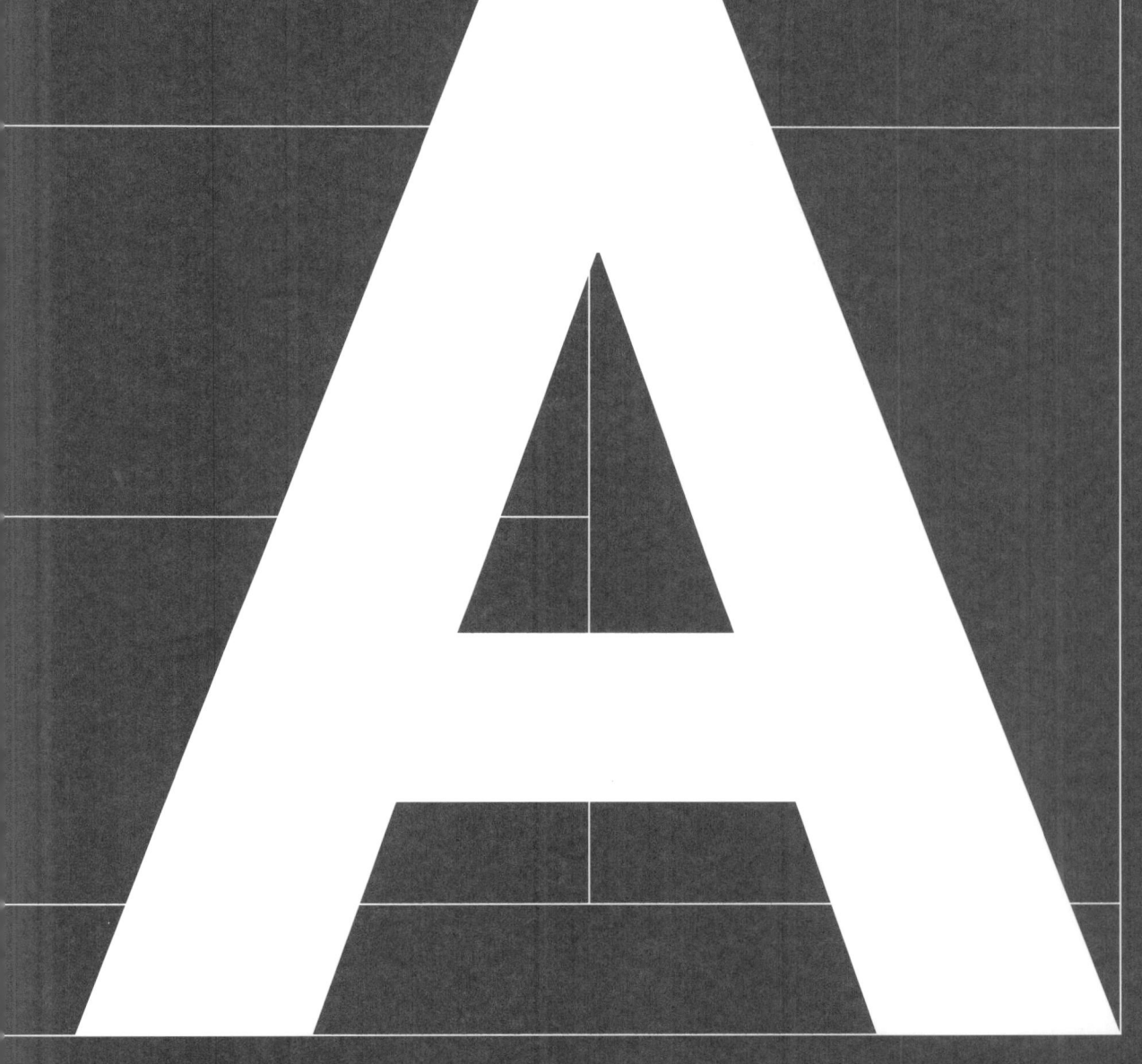

STAN　　SMITH　　"WHITE"　　　　　　　　　　　　　　　　　　　　　　　　　　　　　　　　　　　2011

AN INNOCENT

A CURIOUS

WHO NAMED WHO?

A
is for An Innocent Question

Of all the questions I have been asked, perhaps the most entertaining was from my son Trevor, at age eight, who very innocently asked, "Dad, was the shoe named after you or were you named after the shoe?" – S.S.

Stan Smith shoe illustration by Trevor's son, Austin (age 8). *Opposite:* Trevor Smith playing tennis (age 8).

QUESTION FROM

WHO NAMED WHO? WHO NAMED WHO?

CHILD'S MIND

ALL AROUND

A GLOBAL FOOTPRINT　　　　　　　　　　A GLOBAL FOOTPRINT

WE ARE

THE　　　　　　　　　　　　　　　　　　　　WORLD

A   GLOBAL   FOOTPRINT   A   GLOBAL   FOOTPRINT

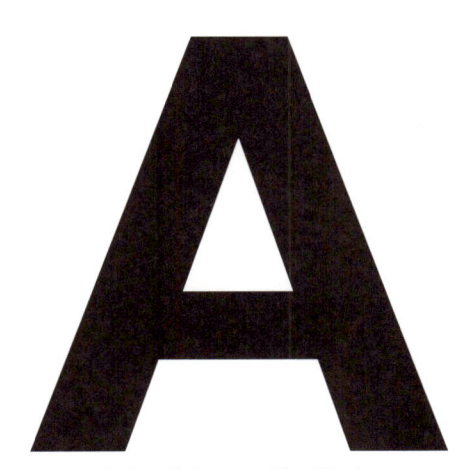

A

is for All Around The World

Tennis has provided a wonderful opportunity to travel the world and meet some fabulous characters. It has made me realize that people share more similarities than differences no matter what their nationality, race, gender, age, culture, or location. The time spent travelling has been enlightening and it is particularly humbling to see that the shoe has been embraced by all. – S.S

The world map in our home represents my love of travel. *Opposite:* Cycling around Honolulu with Arthur Ashe and Bob Lutz, 1969.

THE　　　　　　　　　　　　　　　　　　　　SAME

A GLOBAL FOOTPRINT					A GLOBAL FOOTPRINT

54

Clockwise from top left: Auckland, Barcelona, Ireland, Cairo, Lagos, Hong Kong, Dubai, and The Great Wall of China.

A GLOBAL FOOTPRINT

A GLOBAL FOOTPRINT

A GLOBAL FOOTPRINT

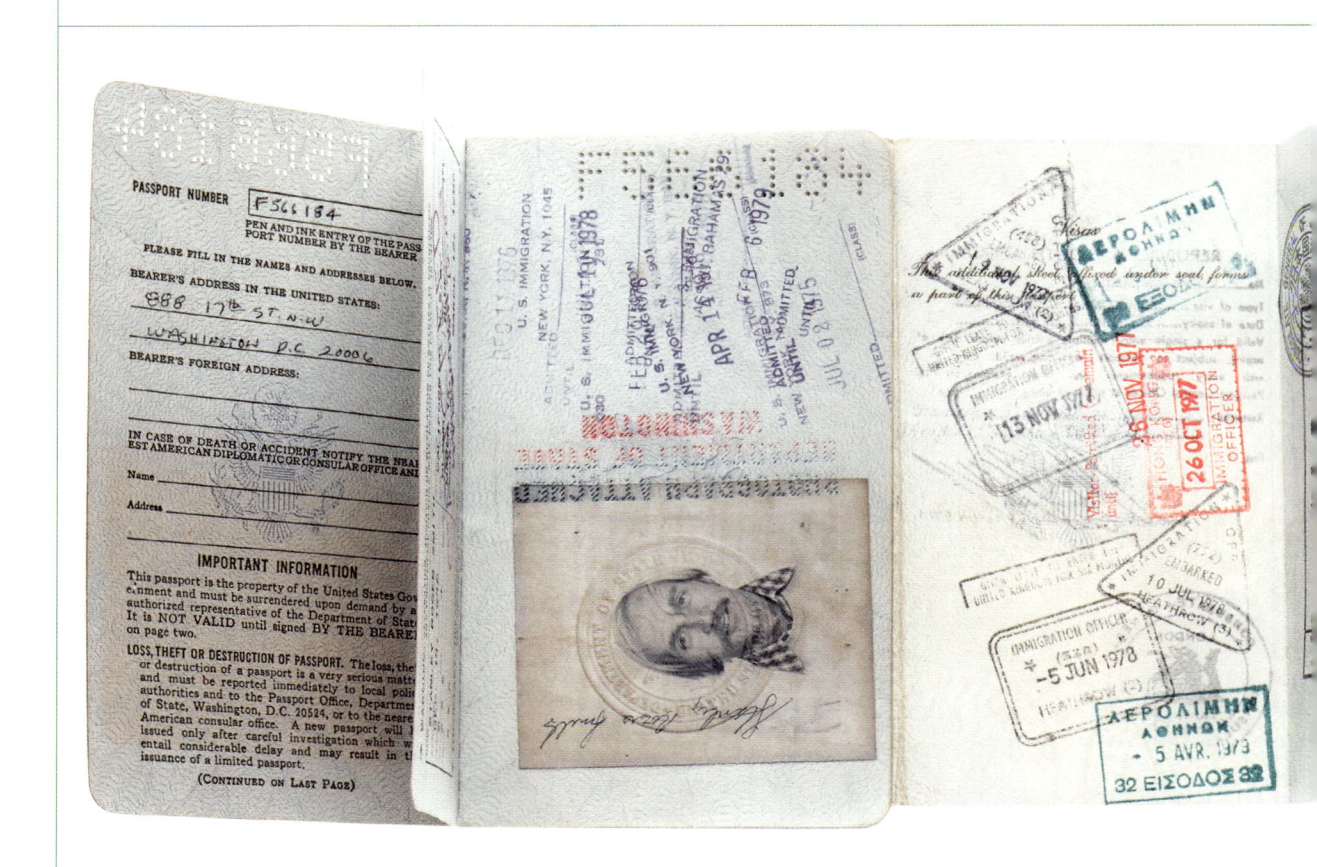

"My first of many passports extensions."
– S.S.

A GLOBAL FOOTPRINT   A GLOBAL FOOTPRINT

ANDROIDS   ALSO

BLADE   RUNNER   BLADE   RUNNER

A
is for Androids

I've seen my shoe being worn by dozens of characters in both international films and television programs over the years. But one of the shoe's most famous appearances might not be a Stan Smith at all. In the classic film *Blade Runner*, the main character played by Harrison Ford chases down fugitive androids wearing what look like black Stan Smiths. But many believe that the shoe is actually a different adidas model, the Official, which resembled the Stan Smith, and was created for sports referees. But nobody is completely certain what shoe he wears, even adidas doesn't know! – S.S.

adidas catalogue, 1975. *Opposite:* Harrison Ford as Rick Deckard in Blade Runner, 1982.

WEARING   THE

DREAM　　　　　　　　　　　　OF

BLADE　RUNNER　　　　　　　　　　　　　　BLADE　RUNNER

STAN　　　　　　　　　　　　SMITH

AN ALL-STAR

CELEBRITY ENDORSEMENT

A
is fo All-Star Endorsement

The idea of "celebrity" sneaker endorsements began in the 1930s. Converse added Chuck Taylor's name to the All Star in 1934 and B. F. Goodrich worked with Jack Purcell in 1935. adidas revived the practice in the postwar era, but its earliest associations were with European athletes whose fame did not speak to the American market. To remedy this, one of the American athletes adidas turned to was the tennis superstar Stan Smith. The combination of crisp design and celebrity endorsement resulted in a sneaker that continues to have relevance within sneaker culture and fashion.

Elizabeth Semmelhack
Senior Curator, Bata Shoe Museum

MAKES EVERYONE

ENDORSEMENT

CELEBRITY ENDORSEMENT

CELEBRITY ENDORSEMENT

Selection of adidas Tennis promotional materials from the 1970s and 1980s.

61

A

STAR

ADIDAS ORIGINALS PHARRELL WILLIAMS

ADIDAS ORIGINALS X PHARRELL WILLIAMS

X   BBC   STAN   SMITH   "PONY   HAIR"   2015

63

X   BBC   STAN   SMITH   "PONY   HAIR"   2015

BUILDING A

FROM HAILLET TO SMITH   FROM HAILLET TO SMITH

64

SHOE STARTED

BETTER TENNIS

FROM HAILLET TO SMITH

B
is for Building a Better Shoe

The concept of what we know as the Stan Smith Shoe was devised even before it had Robert Haillet's name on it—and that goes back into the earliest days of design for the modern sporting shoe. A small team of technicians at adidas were hard at work in 1964 designing the first sporting shoe with leather uppers instead of canvas. After many experimentations, a revolutionary shoe was launched onto the market in 1965 but there was a problem. The sole kept falling off. Having searched for a glue that would hold the shoe together without success, the designers switched to stitching which improved stability and kept the whole thing together.

It was then that Robert Haillet, a Roland Garros semi-finalist and a popular No. 1 in France, was contracted to have his name on the shoe. "There have been many false stories put out about how the shoe was developed," says Martin Herde who heads up the Archives Section at adidas. "But we have done a lot of research and made a big effort to get the facts straight. The first attempt to make a leather sports shoe came in the 1930s but it was not accepted by the market and was dropped. Then, in the 1960s when the Haillet shoe was being developed, adidas was doing the same thing for basketball with the Superstar shoe. The canvas shoes that were being worn for basketball never lasted more than a few games and, despite leather being more expensive, the sport realized that it would be cheaper in the long run to go to leather." In tennis, the Robert Haillet shoe soon proved to be highly popular, not least because of its clean lines. The trademark adidas Three Stripes had been dropped almost at the outset, leaving just the three perforated lines visible on either side. "If the Three Stripes had been left on the shoe, it would never have become the fashion icon it is today," says Herde. "In retrospect, it was a decision that ensured the long term success of the shoe." With the advent of the Haillet shoe, came the additional heel support with the trademark green heel tab.

Opposite: Robert Haillet, the top French player in the late 1950s, had a very creative use for his racket.

WITH GLUE

FROM   HAILLET   TO   SMITH   FROM   HAILLET   TO   SMITH

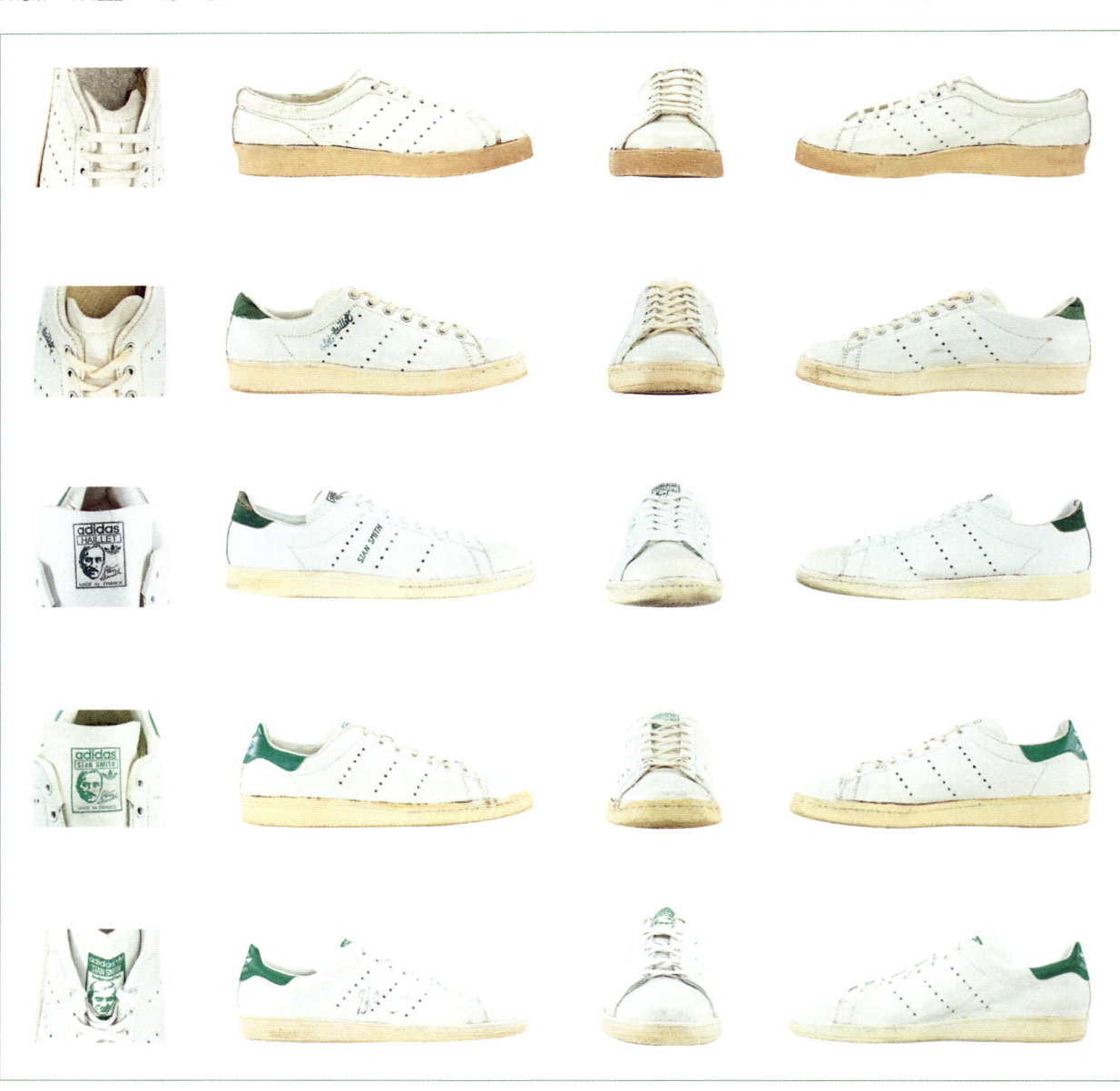

FROM HAILLET TO SMITH   FROM HAILLET TO SMITH

1964

1969

1973

late 1970s

early 1980s

The situation at adidas in the late 1960s had Horst Dassler, son of the company's founder Adi Dassler, running the French operation almost independently from the headquarters in Germany. It was Horst who took the story of the Stan Smith shoe in the direction of the United States. He met Donald Dell, who had a short and successful spell as U.S. Davis Cup captain while at the same time creating his own management company, ProServ. In a master stroke for sales in the America, adidas signed up Dell's entire Davis Cup squad which consisted of Arthur Ashe, Stan Smith, Bob Lutz, and Marty Riessen. "That proved to be unbelievably successful," said Herde. "It hit the market at just the right time during the surge of interest in tennis in the States. But it happened when the shoe was still the Robert Haillet. Stan Smith had not won Wimbledon yet although he appeared in all the catalogues with his Davis Cup colleagues, promoting the Haillet shoe." In 1972, Stan Smith, already the winner of the U.S. Open, did become Wimbledon Champion and, with Haillet on the verge on retirement, adidas realized that a name change would be appropriate. However, Robert's son, Jean-Louis Haillet, himself a professional player for France, points out that there were objections to the change, not from France where the older Haillet continued to be a popular figuré, but from the adidas salesmen in the States.

"They sent the first consignment of Stan Smith shoes back to France because the Haillet had become so popular," said Jean-Louis. "They said it had become established in the shoe trade that 'Haillet means quality' and they didn't want to lose the name." So a compromise was reached. The name Haillet was put back onto what was in the process of becoming the Stan Smith shoe. One can see, on inspecting the tongue of the shoe carrying Smith's likeness, that the name Haillet had been wedged in between Stan's name and his photo. For the next seven years it was marketed that way, satisfying the older generation of Haillet customers. It is ironic that the photograph of Stan Smith, which has appeared on the tongue all these years was taken during the only six months of his life when he was not wearing a moustache. No one quite knows why this has been the case, especially as there exists an image of him made when he was just a member of the Davis Cup squad with the moustache. Sometime in the late 1970s, the moment come when Robert Haillet and adidas came to an agreement to drop his name and the shoe has carried just Stan Smith's insignia and image ever since.

Martin Herde
adidas Archivist
Interviewed by Richard Evans

FROM HAILLET TO SMITH

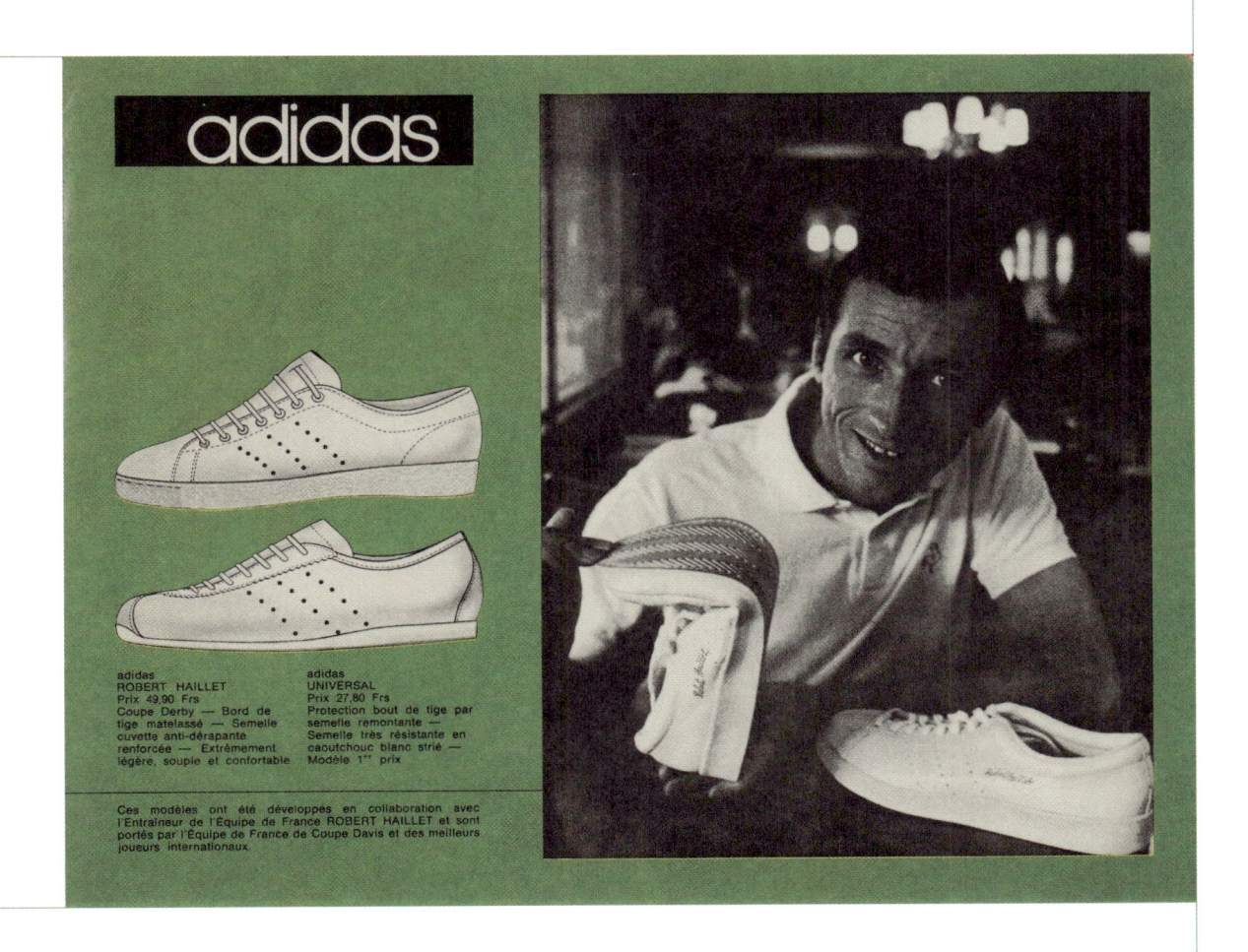

adidas Tennis catalog, Robert Haillet, 1968.

BET YOU CAN'T

LONDON　　　　　　　　　　　　　　　LONDON

B
is for Bet You Can't

I found shoes all over town, but the curve of Regent Street really got my imagination going, so I stalked around it looking for Stans. They were scant enough in that fancy zone that when I finally spotted a pair, I went running. It's crazy chasing shoes, because you have to get crouched down about leprechaun height. When I straightened up after shooting a lady's shoes, there was a bald, bulldog-looking Brit coming right at me with his eyebrow cocked. He asked in a suspicious Scouse, "You're not a weirdo, are ya?" I told him "No, I'm a shoe photographer," and he carried on walking as if I was the thousandth one he'd met.

Daniel Arnold
Photographer

LONDON WITHOUT

WALK　　THROUGH

LONDON　　　　　　　　　　　　　　　　　　　　　LONDON

71

SEEING　　A　　STAN

BROTHER FROM

ARTHUR ASHE

B
is for Brother

I got to know Arthur Ashe when we were on the Davis Cup Team in 1968. In addition to playing together on several teams, we did two State Department tours of Southeast Asia, with the main stop in Vietnam, while he was in the Army. One year we traveled to six African countries together, as I helped him on a Goodwill Tour. – S.S.

My replica of the 14-foot bronze statue of Arthur Ashe at the National Tennis Center in Flushing Meadows, NY.

TEAMMATE FROM

ANOTHER   MOTHER

ARTHUR   ASHE   ARTHUR   ASHE

Arthur Ashe and me sporting our bowlers, umbrellas, and Davis Cup jackets, trying to look like English gentlemen, 1969.

ANOTHER   SCHOOL

ADIDAS X RAF SIMONS

ADIDAS X RAF SIMONS

STAN   SMITH   COMFORT   "RED"   2017

75

STAN   SMITH   COMFORT   "RED"   2017

CAN THREE

LIVE   FOREVER

C

is for Can Three Simple Lines

Jon Wexler grew up with three main interests in life: basketball, sneakers, and hip-hop. By following his dream and working hard to achieve his goals, Wexler has ended up as adidas VP of Global Entertainment and Influencer Marketing.

"Amazingly, it's a job that enables me to encompass all my interests," Wexler says. "Obviously adidas is involved in basketball and makes sneakers, but we are trying new things that some people may not even understand, like thinking of brands becoming record labels."

LIVE   FOREVER

That is a whole story in itself, but Wexler has a relatively simple explanation as to why the sneaker has become such an integral part of modern culture. "Sneakers offer the quickest way for people to project who they are. They are a statement about yourself. The amazing thing about the Stan Smith shoe is that it works for so many people, no matter if they a living in the suburbs of your local town to international cities like New York, London, and Tokyo. They can be considered cool by anyone who wants to wear them."

Jon Wexler, 2014. *Opposite:* Pharrell Williams Hu Holi Stan Smith MC, White & Yellow, 2017. *Far right:* adidas Originals X Pharrell Williams Stan Smith 'Small Polka Dot', 2014.

LINES   LIVE

SIMPLE   CLEAN

LIVE   FOREVER   LIVE   FOREVER

Wexler considers that the way other brands have tried to emulate the Stan Smith is the highest form of flattery. "The simple, clean line is what attracts people all over the world and it can live forever."

Jon Wexler
adidas VP of Global Entertainment and Influencer Marketing
Interviewed by Richard Evans

FOREVER?

COLORFUL   PERSONALITY

COLORS

C

is for Call Of Duty

Maybe because I didn't display a lot of antics on the court people didn't realize I had a colorful personality and sense of humor. Although the originals were white with a little green, I have really enjoyed the color that has been introduced into the line. I actually bought a pair of black shoes in Florence—the first time I ever saw them in black and the first pair I ever bought. If you have a favorite color, you will find a matching shoe. – S.S.

COLORS

adidas Stan Smith Tactile Green, 2017

adidas Originals x Pharrell Williams Stan Smith BPD Blue Polka Dot, 2015

adidas Originals X Pharrell Williams Stan Smith Yellow/Red Polka Dot, 2015

adidas Originals x Pharrell Williams Stan Smith 4-14 Red Solid Pack, 2014

A   SERIOUS

IS   HIDDEN   BEHIND

COLORS   COLORS

adidas Stan Smith, Brown/Orange, 2017

adidas Originals X Pharrell Williams Stan Smith SLD, 2014

adidas Stan Smith Camo, 2017

adidas Stan Smith "Fcotwear White", 2016

Pharrell Williams Hu Holi Stan Smith, Red, 2017

adidas Stan Smith, "Mint", 2018

adidas Stan Smith Shoe Black, 2014

adidas Stan Smith Crystal Speckle, 2016

adidas Originals X Pharrell Williams X BBC Stan Smith Palm Tree Red, 2016

adidas x Pharrell Williams Hu Holi Stan Smith Shoes, Blue, 2018

adidas Stan Smith, Solar Yellow, 2018

adidas Stan Smith Shoes Unisex Gold White, 2017

GAME   FACE

COLLABORATE WITH

HIDEAKI   YOSHIHARA   MRS.   YOKIKO   ODE

adidas Originals x HYKE Stan Smith
"Snakeskin", 2015

LIKE AND YOU

WHOM YOU

HIDEAKI YOSHIHARA MRS. YOKIKO ODE

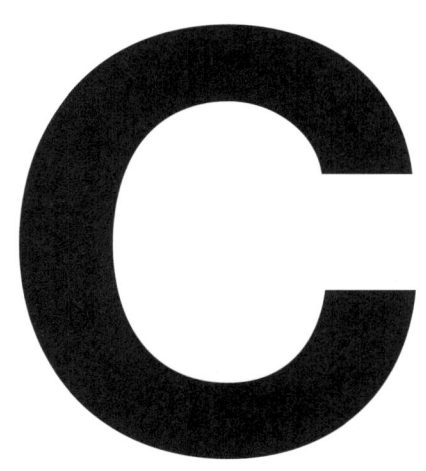

C

is for Collaborate

Ode: When I was a teenager, I used to like Superstar and then shifted to Gazelle but now I wear Stan Smiths. It's my favorite and I believe that Stan Smith is the most wearable sneaker. I love the simple design and ventilation function. Yoshihara: We only collaborate with brands that we have sympathy with, so I don't feel any challenges. Our essential aspect in collaboration is to love the product of our partners. There is a saying, "What one likes, one will do well with." You can add your thoughts to the creation even though it is business. The Stan Smith is so popular because it has the balance that many creators strive for—a minimal design with character.

The Stan Smith is so popular because it has the balance which many creators are striving for – a minimal design with character.

Hideaki Yoshihara and Mrs. Yokiko Ode
Founders and Designers of Hyke

WILL DO WELL

CALL OF

U.S.　ARMY   U.S.　ARMY

C

is for Call Of Duty

I was drafted into the Army on December 16, 1970. They wanted me to represent the U.S. by playing in the Davis Cup competition as well as doing clinics and exhibitions at Army bases, clubs, and intercity venues. I did play and went on to win the Armed Forces Interservice tournament and my superior in charge of the Army tennis team said, tongue-in-cheek, that if I didn't win I would not play Wimbledon—now that's pressure! – S.S.

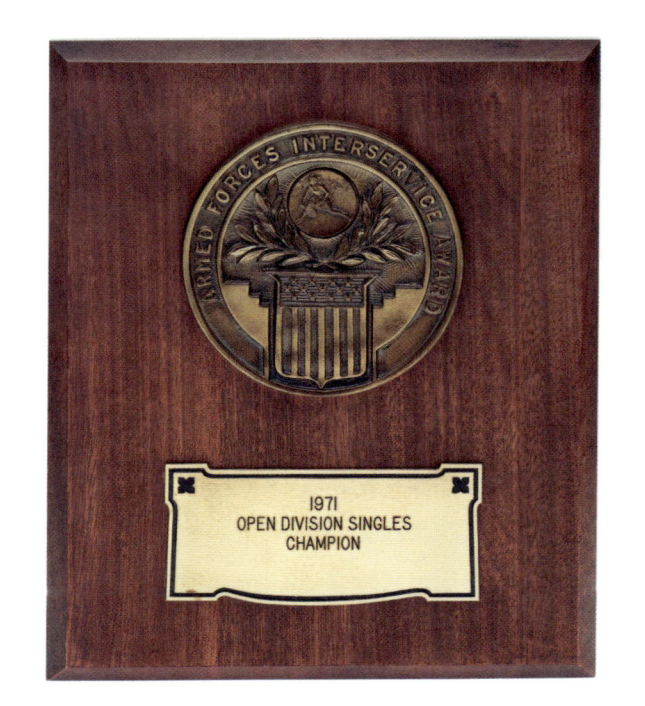

82

One of my more important trophies.
Opposite: I was proud to be in the Army.

THE PRESSURE

DUTY: WHEN

U.S. ARMY   U.S. ARMY

Stan Smith, a 3-year Davis Cupper is now

The Army's Top Tennis Tactician

SFC Carl Martin
Photos by LTC Bob Chick

STAN SMITH was not made for tennis. He appears too big for the fast-moving sport. His lanky 6'4" frame would seem to be more at home on a basketball court or as a fleet tight end in football. That's the impression you get—until you see him play tennis.

When the native Californian takes the court he protects his side of the net with the agility of a cat. He has the starting moves of a champion sprinter and the lateral moves of a much smaller man. A tennis racket in his hand becomes a living extension of his long arm and he uses it as skillfully as a surgeon does a scalpel. Three consecutive years on America's winning Davis Cup team is testimony to the ability of the 24-year-old soldier who recently finished basic training at Fort Ord, Calif.

In addition to his Davis Cup action, the University of Southern California graduate has traveled extensively with Arthur Ashe on the worldwide tennis circuit and conducted hundreds of tennis clinics for youngsters. It may sound like a big fun thing but it can also be a grueling experience. Smith told SOLDIERS, "While Ashe and I were on tour we played in six different countries in just 3 weeks."

When asked how it feels to play against Ashe and other tennis greats the personable athlete says, "It's tough to play at this level of competition. These guys don't allow you a mistake. They jump on your imperfections and take advantage of any error—and there goes your game."

What about the tough Australian competition? "I wish those guys would retire," says Smith with his ever-present smile.

The articulate volleyer began his tennis career at age 14. Three years later he had mastered the game and took the National Junior Championship.

The following years were spent polishing his game and working on his speed to overcome his disadvantage of size. "I was clumsy," Smith admits of his early tennis days. Obviously he overcame it. He was ranked No. 1 in the U.S. last year. And just before entering the Army he beat Rod Laver of Australia in the World Masters Tournament held in Tokyo, pocketing $15,000 for his efforts. Laver is ranked No. 1 in the world by many tennis experts. Smith says his goal in tennis is to become "the best in the world."

Queried about his immediate plans the towering private shrugs and says he has no plans at this time. "The Army is making my plans for me. I'll go where they say and do what they want. If events permit I want to play on the Army tennis team and then go on to interservice competition. I'll have to wait and see."

It's his modest way of saying he's at the top level in tennis and wants to stay there. "You have to be at the top of your game when you play men like Ashe, Laver and others," explains Smith. "Tournament play helps keep that tone."

Whatever the case, it's a good bet that tennis fans will hear more of the big blond competitor as he smashes, volleys, forehands and serves in his scramble to be ranked No. 1 in the world.

16

SOLDIERS

83

IS ON

ADIDAS   ORIGINALS   X   DIESEL

FOR SUCCESSFUL LIVING

ADIDAS   ORIGINALS   X   DIESEL

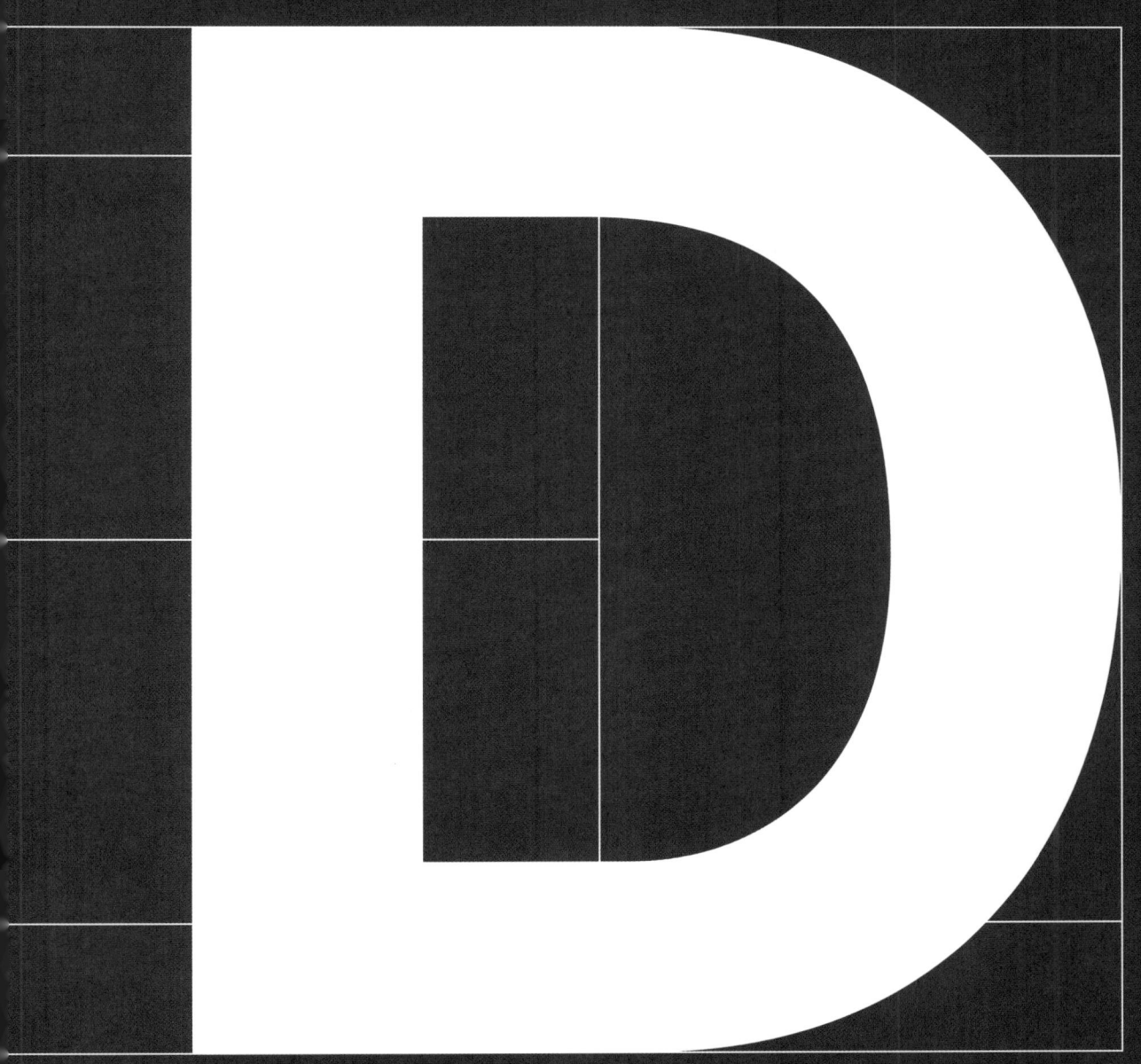

STAN   SMITH   2011

D

85

STAN   SMITH   2011

DOES A RACKET

RACKETS

D

is for Does A Racket

I got my first new racket when I was twelve and it was a Wilson Jack Kramer. In those days in America virtually every top player used the Wilson Kramer. Little did I know that twelve years later I would have my own Wilson Signature racket. I played with that racket for many years, until the wood racket became obsolete and new metal, fiberglass, and graphite materials took over. Jack's stature and fame ensured that his racket would go on selling but Don Budge, Tony Trabert, Barry McKay, and others all had their Wilson Signature rackets at one time or another. – S.S.

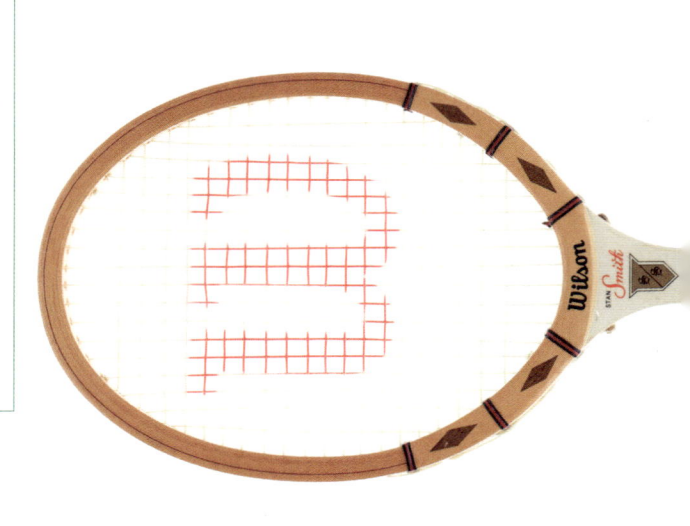

Top: In my Davis Cup outfit with my Wilson Stan Smith autograph racket, which I used in the early 70s when I was ranked No. 1 in the world.

ME SERVE

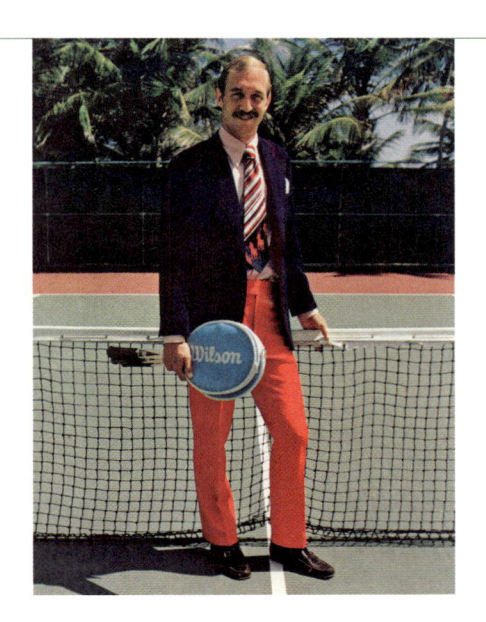

LIKE THIS MAKE

RACKETS　　　　　　　　　　　　　　　　　　　　　　　RACKETS

LIKE STAN?

RACKETS

In 1977 several players and I went on a Goodwill Tour to China. You could tell the Chinese players were behind the times regarding tennis dress and technology, as they all wore white shirts, white shorts, white canvas shoes, and played with wooden tennis rackets. Valerie Ziegenfuss, a member of the U.S. squad, was 5' 10", wore a black sequined dress, blue adidas Billie Jean King tennis shoes, and used an oversized aluminum Prince tennis racket. The Chinese fans thought she might be from Mars! At the end of the tour, the number 1 Chinese player and I exchanged rackets. The Chinese liked to use western names for their products, hence the Aeroplane racket and tennis balls.

The gift racket and can of balls from 1977.

After leaving Wilson I played with an innovative Fischer racket made in Austria. They were new in the racket business but were great technicians and made fantastic skis. The racket played well and the newer versions were bigger and even better. It was always very distinctive in shape and playability. – S.S.

I liked my Fischer Stan Smith autograph racket, even though its shape was unconventional.

DETAILS ARE YOU PLAY

DIDI ROJAS

D
is for Details

I remember immediately being drawn to the green. The person in front of me walking out of the subway steps was wearing Stan Smiths. Ever since that moment, four years ago, I became aware of how many Stan Smiths I saw around the city. My interest in sculpting ceramic shoes started with sneakers after I began to notice how popular specific ones were around New York and Brooklyn. Stans, I noticed, were worn in so many different ways by so many different people. They are not only popular with millennials but with all crowds. They have become my everyday shoe.

DIDI ROJAS

In making the Stan sculptures, it's been incredible how the project I began just a few years earlier has come full-circle. It felt like an amazing way to honor one of my very first ceramic shoe pieces. I modeled the ceramic Stan Smiths off my very own pair. In sculpting the sneakers at two different scales, I felt like I was able to appreciate the crazy amount of detail that goes into their design. All of the pieces were handmade using the coiling method in ceramics. I started off building each one by first making a clay sole and adding more of the material in coils to make the silhouette of the shoe. After the silhouettes were built, I detailed each of the shoes to give them their Stan Smith characteristics. Carving in the adidas logo; painting the legend Stan Smith's

IMPORTANT WHEN ON CLAY

face and signature; poking the holes from the sides of the sneakers; and weaving the laces were a few of the many steps taken to complete every single piece.

The pieces were then dried, glazed, and afterwards fired in a ceramic kiln. Although making clay shoes is probably very different than actual shoes, I felt like I got an insider's look into their making through my own process. I wanted the versions I made, both large and small, to look like they were ceramic but also to stay true to the real Stan Smith sneakers. This project was a huge dream come true for me, not only because I got to do what I love, but also because the Stan Smith means a lot to me.

Didi Rojas
Artist

DIDI ROJAS

Stan Smith ceramic sculpture, 2018

DAVIS CUP

BUCHAREST

D

is for Davis Cup

The early 1970s coincided with the heyday of those two Romanian rogues, Ion Tiriac and Ilie Nastase, both brilliant players in their very different ways and both a nightmare to play against. Orchestrated by Tiriac, who is now thought to be the richest man in Romania (he could do more than wield a tennis racket), they thought up every trick in the book to stretch, bend, and contort the rules. Strong referees and umpires were needed to keep them in check, but such officials were in short supply in those days and we were frequently caught on the wrong side of some shocking decisions.

ALWAYS ARRIVE TO

PLAYERS DIDN'T

BUCHAREST

BUCHAREST

A WARM WELCOME

BUCHAREST   BUCHAREST

With home court advantage, we managed to beat Romania 5–0 in Cleveland in 1969 and 3–2 in Charlotte in 1971, but the final of 1972 was something else. We had to travel to Bucharest to face Tiriac, Nastase (who had just beaten Arthur Ashe in the U.S. Open final), and a stadium full of screaming, chanting Romanians, all whipped into a fury at the behest of Tiriac. A formidable figure on any day of the week, with his black curly hair and huge moustache, Tiriac was impossible and it was years before we started talking to each other again!

The tennis was not the only problem we had to deal with in Bucharest. It was the year of the Olympic massacre in Munich and the security blanket we were subjected to was suffocating. It was all the more intense because two of our team, Harold Solomon and Brian Gottfried, were Jewish. We had two massive security guards, Bill and George, one of whom was Karate champion of Eastern Europe, and there were armed guards on the seventeenth floor of the InterContinental hotel. No one without a pass was allowed up there. We saw people in their bathrobes actually being ejected from their rooms and moved to a different floor. We all felt claustrophobic and Solly, in particular, hated the constant proximity of the guards. He complained and they backed off for a few days until the police thought they had discovered someone who

Top: Examining a ball mark at a crucial stage in the match. *Bottom:* One of my favorite shots. *Opposite:* Ion Tiriac attempting to stop a referee from examining a ball mark.

wanted to attack us and they clamped down again. The whole thing was very nerve-racking.

Pumped by the ecstatic adulation of the crowd, Tiriac won the first set of this crucial match, using that shoveled forehand of his to good effect, moving well and volleying impressively. Once again, the atmosphere was intimidating. The body guards were back in action and there were armed soldiers around the stadium. For my part, there was only one thing to do: attack. So, I clicked into aggressive gear and, fortunately, didn't miss much. Tiriac was still playing at a high level but I was matching him now and took the second set.

I went up 5–3 in the third set but lost my serve. Tiriac served at 4–5 and I batted the ball away to the ball boy when his first delivery missed the line. But the line judge was staring at the sky or something and the umpire called 15–0. From then on, I played everything I could reach. He then hit a serve long—no call—and my good return was called out. I got a little bit crazy. None of our team had been very confident that we could win in Bucharest and I was beginning to see why. But I got to my ad-set point, and I hit a good backhand down the line. Tiriac said something to the service linesman in Romanian, and he suddenly stood up and called out! Tiriac promptly served the second serve into the net and I won the third set 6–4, lost the fourth 6–2, and then found everything easier as Tiriac wilted. I closed it out 6–0.

So, we could, and did, win in Bucharest, but it had been a bitter battle and when I went up to shake hands with Tiriac, I told him I couldn't respect him as a person. I think he was shocked. But then something strange happened: when I appeared on court for the presentation ceremony, the crowd, so hostile for three days, started applauding me. It began quite slowly and the sound grew until they were giving me a really big ovation. I was surprised and moved. It was something I never expected. – S.S.

THE BATTLE OF BUCHAREST

Thirty years ago, one month after the Munich Olympics, the U.S. Davis Cup team flew to Romania for the first-ever final behind the Iron Curtain. It would be a weekend that no one involved could ever forget. By Peter Bodo

PHOTOGRAPHS BY RUSS ADAMS

Davis Cup memories of Bucharest, Tennis magazine, 2002.

ADIDAS   ORIGINALS

STAN   SMITH   CROC   "INK   BLUE"   2017

STAN   SMITH   CROC   "INK   BLUE"   2017

EASE INTO

AND STEP

COLETTE

E
is for Ease

Q: How does the Stan Smith shoe fit with what Colette had to offer?
Sarah Andelman: It fit perfectly. It's the essence of what we wanted to offer: something authentic, pure, and powerful!

Q: How and when did you first become aware of the Stan Smith shoe as something other than a tennis shoe?
S.A.: I can't even remember. It has always been an iconic style for me.

COLETTE

Q: Why did it appeal to your customers?
S.A.: I think everybody recognizes the Stan Smith and can adopt it. It's so easy to wear, so comfortable . . . It's like the white tee of the sneakers game.

Q: How did a sports shoe make the transition to a fashion item on a worldwide scale?
S.A.: It's easy, with style!

Q: How long do "fashion fads" last?
S.A.: That's the beauty of the Stan Smith: it's timeless, it's beyond fashion. It can be trendy with a special treatment, but the original will always remain a classic.

adidas Originals x Colette Stan Smith, 2014.

YOUR STYLE

COLETTE COLETTE

Q: Do you see even more longevity for the Stan Smith shoe?
S.A.: Absolutely, we always need some landmarks.

Q: What is your perspective on the business of selling a fashion item and why it appeals to customers? Compared with other designs and companies you have worked with, how easy has it been to collaborate with the Stan Smith shoe?
S.A.: adidas has always been a great to work with, and I have nice memories of one of our first sneaker collabs we did: the Adicolor by Claude Closky, in 2005. And of course, doing a Stan Smith was a huge honor. I kept it very simple, with just blue dots and the launch, in the presence of Mr. Stan Smith himself at Colette, was a very special and moving moment I'll remember forever!

Q: Why has it been easier than some, if this is the case?
S.A.: Great team!

Sarah Andelman
Founder of Colette, Paris

BEYOND FASHION

EQUAL TALENT

MARGIE   GENGLER   SMITH

E
is for Equal Talent

I grew up in a large family of five girls and two boys on Long Island. My parents encouraged us to participate in many sports; however, the girls gravitated to tennis. Ivy League schools started going coed in the early 1970s, and I was thrilled to be admitted to Princeton's Class of 1973—the first class of women. It was particularly special for me because my grandfather and father were Princeton graduates, and they never dreamed a female would follow in their footsteps.

The first intercollegiate women's sport at Princeton was tennis, and I played in the number-one position. Needless to say, our team received much attention as

Margie Smith on the cover of Princeton Alumni Weekly, 1973. *Opposite:* Eastern Tennis Association Hall of Fame Trophy, 2004.

THE BIG

RUNS IN SMITH FAMILY

MARGIE GENGLER SMITH

we dominated our opponents and proved that coeds could be athletic.

During this time Stan and I dated, and he occasionally showed up on campus. After the historic Bobby Riggs vs. Billie Jean King Battle of the Sexes, the women's varsity and men's junior varsity teams had a competition. Stan umpired my match and later confessed that he had a difficult time being neutral.

In May 1973 a picture of me holding my Stan Smith Wilson racquet and wearing my white letter sweater (which is awarded to the captain of an undefeated team) appeared on the cover of the Princeton Alumni Weekly with the label "Princeton's Best Athlete." I certainly was not the best athlete, but I was the face of Princeton's pioneering women athletes.

Margie Smith
Stan's wife and tennis champion

EDBERG   JUNIOR

STEFAN   EDBERG   STEFAN   EDBERG

E
is for Edberg

I was walking away from Wimbledon on Church Road in 2017 with my son Christoff. Christoff was wearing the Stan Smith shoes and Stan walked up from behind, surprising us as he mentioned that he liked the shoes. Christoff thought it was pretty funny that he had the shoes on and Stan was actually there.

Stefan Edberg
Tennis champion

Sweden's Stefan Edberg, former world No. 1. *Opposite:* Stefan Edberg autograph adidas shoe, part of the adidas family.

WEARS   STANS   AT

SEES AND

STEFAN EDBERG · STEFAN EDBERG

STAN SMITH

STEFAN EDBERG

107

THE SAME TIME

ADIDAS X OPENING CEREMONY

108

ADIDAS X OPENING CEREMONY

STAN   SMITH   "WHITE/GREY"   2014

109

STAN   SMITH   "WHITE/GREY"   2014

FIGURING

GEORGE TOLEY GEORGE TOLEY

110

MAKES TENNIS

GEORGE　TOLEY

F

is for Figuring Out

My college coach at USC, George Toley, was an intuitive person who not only knew what to say, but when to say it. And he knew when to get a young player to pull back and use some judgment. On one occasion in San Antonio at the NCAA Championships in 1968, Toley found himself in the awkward position of being coach to both Bob Lutz and myself when we were playing each other in the final. He didn't want to be seen offering advice to one and not the other so, at one stage, he walked casually past the back of my chair at a change over and muttered, "Might consider not coming into the net on every shot." – S.S.

Opposite: George Toley, my USC coach, giving me post-college tips, 1975.

FOR THE

MARK   MATHABANE

F
is For the Human Race

When I met Stan in the fall of 1977, I was filled with hatred for white people, because of the life I had led under racism and oppression in South Africa, and because of the many friends I had lost, including my girlfriend, who'd been shot and killed by soldiers and the police during the 1976 Soweto student rebellion. Tennis was the only thing that kept me alive and sane. As a tennis player I knew about the iconic sneaker, but little about the man, except that he was friends with Arthur Ashe, who'd inspired me to learn the game. Ashe was the first free black man I'd ever seen when he came to South Africa in 1973 to play in a tournament,

MARK   MATHABANE

Mark Mathabane's family visiting the Smith's home, 1992. *Opposite:* Mark and Stan at the US Open, 1981.

BOTH ON AND

HUMAN RACE

MARK MATHABANE

MARK MATHABANE

OFF THE COURT

MARK MATHABANE

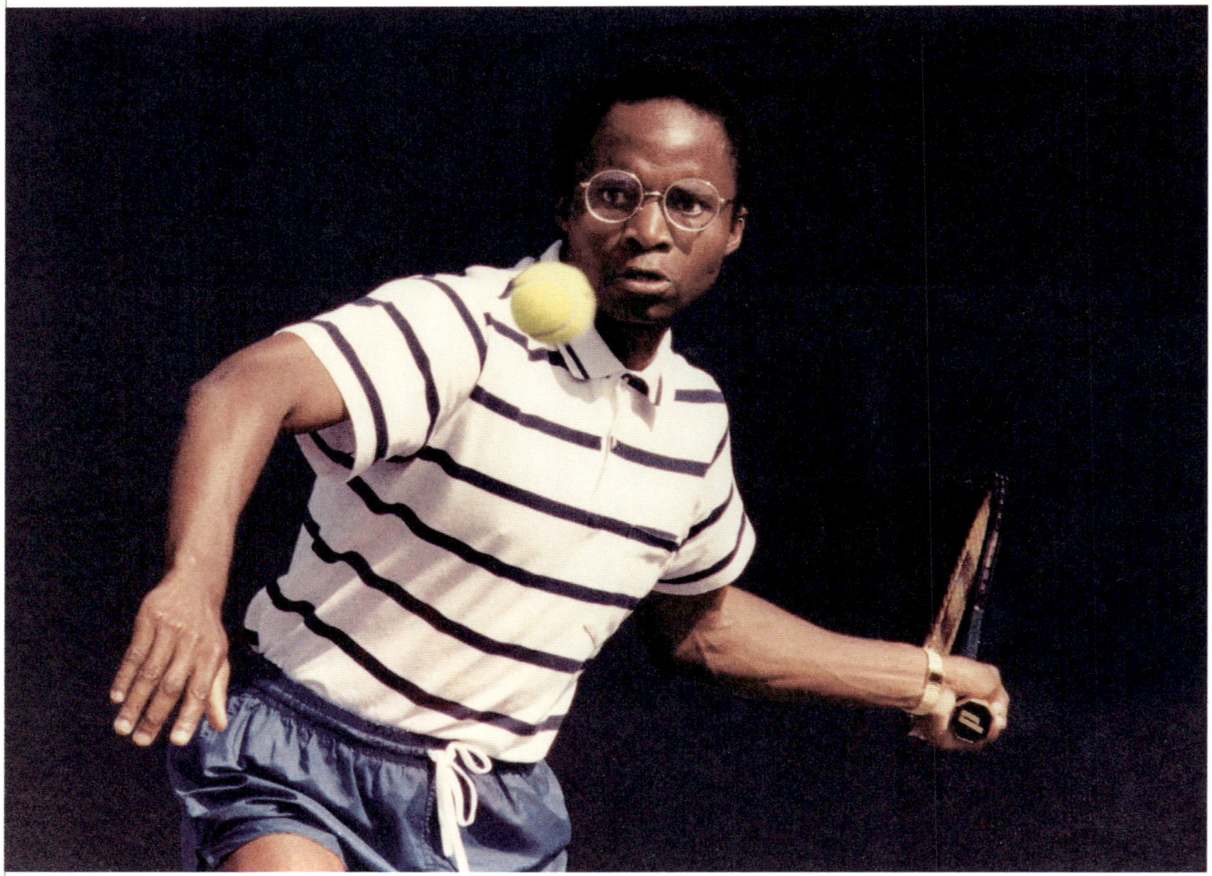

which he'd demanded be integrated for the first time in its history.

From the outset, talking to Stan made me realize why his sneaker had such global appeal. It embodied the character and soul of man. Stan had the uncanny ability to spontaneously relate to anyone—regardless of color, race, religion, creed, nationality, or sexual orientation—as a fellow human being. His sneaker was the perfect metaphor for enabling those who wore it to be able to walk in the shoes of anyone they met—provided they had the courage, like Stan did, to be human even with total strangers.

In the culture of my Venda tribe, to which the current president of South Africa, Cyril Ramaphosa, belongs, there's no greater honor to bestow on someone than to name your child after them, as a reflection of what is most admirable and inspiring about that person. That's why I was most proud when my wife and I named our youngest child Stanley, in remembrance of the miracle the man with the iconic shoe had wrought in my life after our chance meeting. Some may call it destiny. I call it the Stan Smith effect. If Stan had not walked in my shoes and felt my pain as a fellow human being after I had shared with him and his wife, Margie, the story of growing up poor and black in Alexandra, one of the worst ghettos in the world, I would be dead and buried alongside so many of my friends and comrades.

Through Stan I got a tennis scholarship to America, where I graduated from college with honors, went on to write a bestselling memoir, *Kaffir Boy*, which has inspired young people around the world to always have hope, to believe in themselves, and to never give up on their dreams, no matter how impossible they may seem. Not only that, but I became the proud father of three children who all attended Princeton, when I was the first member in my family to go to school. Through tennis I was fortunate to meet the human being behind the iconic sneaker, who taught me the true meaning of empathy, which is sorely needed in our world today and is key to our collective survival as a species.

Finally, I've lost count of how many readers of my memoir of all ages—but especially the young of every

Tennis was the only thing which kept me alive and sane.

Opposite: A young Mark Mathabane during his time post college, 1989.

Some may call it destiny. I call it the Stan Smith effect.

race, religion, and socio-economic background—have written me since my book was published in 1986 to say how much they loved the Stan Smith sneaker. They had no inkling it was connected to such a caring human being who gave me the second chance the country of my birth had cruelly denied me, because of the color of my skin, to fulfill my potential while helping others as best I can. I always take the opportunity to respond to as many of these letters and e-mails as possible, so I can emphasize this salient point, which I hope you will glean from reading Stan's book.

Stan and his sneaker, I believe, teach us, especially in these trying times of wars and divisions, that there's only one race that ultimately matters in the annals of history—the human one. That's why the Stan Smith sneaker is popular all over the world, and has the power to bring people together, to celebrate the best in every culture and in all of us, through music, art, sports, film, dance, and fashion. This is a sign of true love, the universal language of the human heart, which we must all have the courage to speak if we are to save ourselves from ourselves and create a better future for all people.

Mark Mathabane
Author and collegiate tennis player

Jeanne and Arthur Ashe, Mark and Gail, Stan and Margie, New York City, 1988. *Opposite:* Mark ringing in the 1993 New Year with Stan and Margie, and Chelsea and Bill Clinton.

FAVORITE　　　　STANS

FAVORITES　　　　　　　　　　　　　　　　　FAVORITES

F

is for Favorite Stans

These are my most-treasured Stan Smiths over the years, but not necessarily in order. Of course, my favorite is the iconic one without which there would be no others. I have always been partial to the Nubuck or suede, like the black suede pair that I designed for my wife and myself. The limited edition Nastase-Smith is special and the Horween leather is like a glove. I enjoy mixing it up and trying on the different models. – S.S.

adidas Stan Smith, 2014

adidas Stan Smith Vintage "Smith vs. Nastase", 2006

Stan Smith, "mi adidas", 2009

adidas Originals X Pharrell Williams Stan Smith "Jacquard", Gold 2014

FROM　　　　　　THE

OF ALL TIME

FAVORITES   FAVORITES

adidas Stan Smith BOOST PK, 2014

adidas Originals x Horween Stan Smith Leather Tan, 2015

adidas Stan Smith White/Orange, 2018

Adidas Stan Smith "Midsummer Metallic" Pack, Gold Met, 2015

adidas Originals Stan Smith "Pastel Pack", Icey Blue, 2017

adidas Stan Smith "Battle Pack" World Cup, 2014

Baby Stan Smith, 2008

adidas Originals X Pharrell Williams Stan Smith 'Jacquard', Navy 2014

adidas Stan Smith II "Kermit the Frog", 2006

adidas Stan Smith Zig Zag Pack Red, 2016

adidas Originals Stan Smith "Pastel Pack", Tactile Rose, 2017

Adidas Stan Smith Boost Metallic (Silver / White), 2017

MAN   HIMSELF

ADIDAS   ORIGINALS   X   PHARRELL   WILLIAMS

120

ADIDAS   ORIGINALS   X   PHARRELL   WILLIAMS

STAN   SMITH   SPD   "POLKA   DOT"   PACK   2014

STAN   SMITH   SPD   "POLKA   DOT"   PACK   2014

GUESS WHAT

STAN SMITH EVENTS

STAN SMITH EVENTS

Stan with rugby legend Jonah Lamu and Gary Niebur at the Rugby World Cup, New Zealand, 2011.

GUESTS ASK

ALL THE TO GET?

STAN SMITH EVENTS

G

is for Guess What

My first encounter with Stan was during the Davis Cup final in 1972, when I was a ball boy, but we met formally in 1983 when I was playing on the ATP Tour and through an organization called Young Life. In 1993, we formed a business relationship to host a corporate event at Wimbledon and the feedback was, "I've been coming to Wimbledon for 30 years, but never like this."

The business relationship became a partnership we named Stan Smith Events, with the vision to provide exclusive celebrity-hosted experiences. Since 1993, we have been fortunate enough to host leaders from all over the world and many Fortune 500 companies at some of the most premier global sporting events. The common denominator through all of these events has been Stan Smith as the celebrity host and his shoes as a talking point and gift for the guests.

Thousands of guests have received the shoes, some at the foot of their bed in place of the hotel slippers, at events ranging from the Tennis Grand Slams to Rugby and FIFA World Cups, the Olympics to Super Bowls, among others. The shoes have been given to commemorate the most special of moments for clients and friends, including baby shoes to expectant parents. They've also been sent as a "thank you note" following important client meetings. And where else in the world can you get a pair of Stan Smith shoes, signed by Stan Smith right in front of you? It is that moment, combined with the moment when Stan tells the story of the shoe and its relaunch that prompts guests to take out their phone and take pictures and videos. And it is that bespoke experience that we have strived to deliver to our clients over the years–thus the relationship with the Stan Smith shoe and our company has been constant. Likewise, on a personal note, I've become connected to the shoe–owning over 30 pairs personally as well as many more among my family. I've seen a lot of history of the shoe lived out through Stan and I'm grateful for the relationships to both the man and the shoe.

Gary Niebur
President, Stan Smith Events

GET RID

ALMOST INVISIBLE   ALMOST INVISIBLE

G
is for Get Rid of Everything

In the late 1960s, when adidas designers set out to produce a leather tennis shoe to be worn by world-class players, they made a decision that helped create history. They decided to make the Three Stripes, which were emblazoned over every adidas item as the company's trademark—almost invisible.

The Three Stripes are on both sides of the shoe, but you have to look closely to detect the perforations in the leather. Paul Gaudio, who is now in charge of 650 designers for adidas worldwide, spoke to some of the people involved in that decision when he first worked for adidas in 1991.

"They were looking for something universal and low-key," says Gaudio. "They were attempting to be different and wanted to get away from bold athletic branding. And, of course, they succeeded. Designers can only fantasize about creating something that simple and that memorable. The clean simplicity of the Stan Smith shoe, as it became known, enabled it to become what it is today: a fashion icon."

As he leads his army of designers in today's rapidly changing world, Gaudio emphasizes three essential points: One, the design must be born from the culture in which it lives. Two, the item must be designed for a purpose: Why is it being designed? For what? Is it solving a problem?

adidas Stan Smith, 2014, tongue hole. *Opposite:* adidas Stan Smith, Herbert Hainer Special Edition seeding box, 2014.

TO MAKE ROOM

OF EVERYTHING

ALMOST INVISIBLE ALMOST INVISIBLE

There must be a pure need. All these questions must work in context together with point one. Three, the item must be simple, but not simplistic. It must strip back the clutter and noise and attract the consumer intuitively. As Gaudio points out, you can go too far down the simple road and run the risk of being boring. "That is why it is important to have it derive from something of value. In this instance we are talking about an item worn by a great tennis player, a Wimbledon champion who has brought his own elegance and worth to a shoe that has been accepted by peoples all over the world."

Once again, the question of why the Stan Smith shoe has survived through the ages comes back to design. "Fortuitously, over the past ten years, there has been a swing to a more casual look, reflecting a more casual lifestyle," says Gaudio. "That, of course, has helped the Stan Smith shoe, but it is hard to think of a shift in fashion that wouldn't, which says everything about the design."

Paul Gaudio
adidas Global Creative Director
Interviewed by Richard Evans

FOR EVERYONE

GORMAN SHOWS

TORREMOLINOS   TORREMOLINOS

G
is for Gorman

In 1972, the third "Masters" ever played—following Tokyo and Paris—was held in Barcelona. We knew about Spanish hours but we were still a little amazed to hear that the semifinals would be starting at 10:00 p.m. So, we tried to get into the rhythm by staying up really late when Tom Gorman, Jimmy Connors, and I trained earlier in the week at Torremolinos. It turned out that Ilie Nastase and Connors got through to the first semifinal and Gor and I reached the other. So, I went off for dinner at around 9:00 p.m. and actually got on court just before midnight. Gor was playing really well on the indoor court and led by two sets to one and 7–6 in the fourth. I noticed that he was swinging away, just going for winners and not running after my shots. He caught me with a couple on my serve and reached match point. I turned away and then, as I was about to serve, I noticed him walking towards the umpire. I thought that was strange and, at first glance, I thought he was going to complain about something. We were very good friends and I couldn't believe he was trying a bit of gamesmanship at match point. My instant reaction was to be annoyed, but Tom kept on walking and said something to the umpire, who motioned for me to come the umpire's chair. Then he announced, "Mr. Gorman is defaulting. Game, set, and match to Mr. Smith!" I was stunned. As we shook hands, Gor explained that his back had gone and he knew he wouldn't be able to play the final the following day. As an act of sportsmanship, it was right up there. We were all aware that Commercial Union had become a new and valuable sponsor for the event and Tom was loath to deprive them of a final. – S.S.

Opposite: Tom Gorman had his back problems during the Masters tournament in Barcelona, 1972.

CAN SOMETIMES

THAT BACK PAIN

TORREMOLINOS TORREMOLINOS

Tom Gorman's Selfless Act

Tom Gorman, nearing a possible victory over Stan Smith at the Consumer Union Grand Prix Masters playoff, unexpectedly gave the match away when his back acted up. Rather than wreck finals, Tom withdrew, losing money but gaining esteem. Top right: a former British Davis Cup coach, John Barrett, was pressed into service in an attempt to relieve Gorman's back which was hurt earlier at Wimbledon. Below: a nonplussed Stan Smith watches Gorman withdraw suddenly when the Irishman was match point up. Smith later praised Gorman's action as "a typical example of Tom's character."

LEAD TO GAIN

ADIDAS STAN SMITH

128

ADIDAS STAN SMITH

MISS PIGGY 2006

129

MISS PIGGY 2006

HAGGLE ALL

THE KUWAITIS' BAZAAR

H
is for Haggle

In 1984, I was about twelve years old, and in junior high. I lived in post-revolution Iran, and it was at the middle of the war between Iran and Iraq. There were sirens on the radio at night, lights going off, and fear of aerial bombardments were the norm. There was only one shopping mall in Tehran where you could find the odd Western-style clothing. It was called "The Kuwaitis' Bazaar," which should give you an idea of where the commodities would have likely been smuggled from! A few of my cool schoolmates wore the Stan Smith to school, which they had been given as presents from uncles abroad. I was dying to have a pair too. After weeks of begging my parents, they agreed. So, one winter evening we go to the Kuwaitis' Bazaar, and we asked around to find out which of the shops would have them. Eventually we found one. The shop keeper said he happened to have a pair of Stan Smiths just the right size, which a pilot had just brought from abroad and sold to him. My eyes were shining with glee and longing! He asked five thousand tomans. That's a lot!

My dad says that's too much and offers four thousand. The haggling goes on, in true Iranian bazaar fashion, for what seems ages. I'm holding the shoes in my hand and not willing to let go. Finally, my dad refuses to throw the towel in and says no thank-you. I am horrified! As we leave the shop he winks at me and says it's a tactic; you start walking out and the shopkeeper always asks you to come back at the last minute and agrees with your offered price. I'm sure his trick won't work, and it doesn't. Outside, my dad says, "It's too late. My pride won't let me go back in and pay what he wants." I am devastated, standing in the snow in floods of tears. We go home.

But I did get my pair. We went back the next day, pretending we'd never been before, and this time we didn't haggle!

Pooneh Ghoddoosi
Journalist

DOWN TO

THE WAY

THE KUWAITIS' BAZAAR

AF 1028 STAN SMITH – HAILLET
The Haillet model the most popular tennis shoe in the world. Stan Smith has selected this remarkable shoe for his personal use. Very light and comfortable soft leather uppers form instantly to the contour of the foot. New improved insole for longer wear. Durable adidas-multi-grip sole for excellent footing. Adjustable orthopedic arch support.

AF 1080 NEWCOMBE
New styled Newcombe tennis shoe featuring the adidas polyurethane sole as well as the revolutionary cangoran upper. This breathable upper ensures maximum comfort and optimum performance. Exceptionally comfortable polyurethane sole provides excellent traction. Special toe protection for longer life. One of the lightest tennis shoes ever.

AF 1028

AF 1080

AF 1042

AF 1042 ROD LAVER
Designed in collaboration with Rod Laver. A unique tennis shoe with ventilated nylon uppers. Reinforced nylon material that breathes and allows perspiration to evaporate. Special padding for protection of heel and Achilles tendon. New improved vulcanized gum rubber sole reinforces the ball-of-foot and heel.

adidas catalogue, 1975.

YOUR FEET

HILTON   HEAD

THE LEGEND   THE LEGEND

132

"I have really enjoyed coaching at Smith Stearns Tennis Academy in Hilton Head, SC." – S.S.

TO   A   WORLD   -

IS HOME

THE LEGEND THE LEGEND

H
is for Hilton Head

I met Stan just before Wimbledon in June of 1971, in London, when he showed up at the Pepsi office with his tennis partner, Bob Lutz. He invited us to Wimbledon and I was with him the night he lost to John Newcombe. He told me later that night that he was in the fifth set thinking about the speech, and which music to choose for his first dance with Billie Jean King at that evening's champions ball, and lost concentration. But he made up for it and I was with him and his parents the next year when we watched him triumph at Wimbledon. We see him frequently in Hilton Head, where he has the famous Smith Stearns Tennis Academy for would-be college players and professionals.

He is an amazingly kind, patient, and generous person. He and his wonderful wife, Margie, have dedicated themselves to the Boys & Girls Club for twenty-five years and have helped thousands of young people find a purpose in life.
The shoe came later.
He has grown into an unbelievable legend. Every one of my children and grandchildren wear his shoe, as do millions around the world. It is a fashion icon and most young people I've met have no idea that there is a tennis legend behind the shoe!
May the legend continue.

Tom Kemeny
Family Friend and Former PepsiCo Executive

FAMOUS SNEAKERHEAD

HERE'S A

STAN FANS   STAN FANS

H

is for Here's A Shoe

"I bought them with my mom as a way to celebrate our birthdays since we were born on the same day. We got the exact same model. We thought it was fun to give each other the same present, for the same reason, on the same day. She's my best friend so I'm happy to share this thing with her."

"I first came in contact with the Stan Smith when I was in High School through my Tennis Club. The shoe being so comfortable, I never grew tired wearing it and with the added plus of the shoe being so stylish it's the ideal must-have."

Carlotta Ibba
Student, Rome, Italy

Tei Towa
Musician and DJ, Tokyo, Japan

adidas Stan Smith, White/Green, 2014

LETS YOU

SHOE THAT

STAN FANS STAN FANS

"I was fifteen years old when I received my first Stans and I loved them ever since then. I use one pair four or five times a week, and the others for going out. These sneakers are very popular in Ghana—even in my hometown. I wish I could buy another pair soon, so I am saving the money that I receive from my parents every month. I don't know who Stan Smith is, but I assume he's a great man."

"Stan Smith sneakers have been a wardrobe staple of mine since I was a teenager and that's their brilliance—they timelessly speak to every generation and fashion trend. Their clean design and combination of street, athletic, and classic influences make them unique, cool, and iconic. I have no doubt we'll know and adore the Stan Smith name for decades to come."

Bill White
Student, Accra, Ghana

Karlie Kloss
Supermodel, New York, USA

adidas Stan Smith, White/Red, 2014   adidas Stan Smith, White/Blue, 2014

DO YOU

HARMONY IS

SHIGEKI FUJISHIRO

H

is for Harmony

In the beginning I was attracted by how it was not speaking out too much and how the stripes were designed.

On collaboration: It is important not to destroy our partner's look and respect the limits of how far we can go in collaboration. I believe good collaboration depends on how we can blend each other's flavor and balance.

I never really emphasize Japan. To suggest international design is not to emphasize "Japanese" because I think it is important to create harmony between different countries.

Shigeki Fujishiro
Designer

BALANCE BETWEEN

THE PRECIOUS

SHIGEKI FUJISHIRO   SHIGEKI FUJISHIRO

adidas Consortium x Shigeki Fujishiro
x Stan Smith "PLAY" Pack, 2014.

DIFFERENT FLAVORS

ADIDAS   ORIGINALS   X   HORWEEN

ADIDAS   ORIGINALS   X   HORWEEN

STAN SMITH MID 2015

I LOVE PARIS

is for I Love Paris

Stan Smith, in case you haven't visited in a while, take it from me man, you run Paris. You beat the beret. From the knee down, that is your city. If you want my theory, it's because you took the stripes off. No self-respecting French person could wear that classic banded sailor shirt and a striped shoe. But having the impression of stripes? Mmwah, that's formidable. I found packs of Stans skipping up the Sacre Couer steps, dragging across a cobblestone Île Saint-Louis courtyard, smoothing on the Comptoir Général dance floor, under the Eiffel Tower, over the canal and through as many gardens as I could get to. Can you tell I'm a tourist?

Daniel Arnold
Photographer

PARIS LOVES

AS MUCH AS

PARIS PARIS

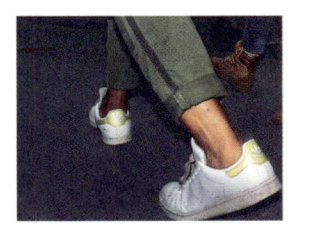

STAN SMITH

I GREW UP PLAYING

ONE THING STAYED THE SAME　　　　　　　　　　ONE THING STAYED THE SAME

I

is for I Grew Up

I moved back to New York in 1987 and it wasn't a pretty sight. People nowadays often romanticize the graffiti-festooned subways, the grit, the old Times Square. But here's the deal: the subways sucked, you got mugged all the time,[1] and if you were a real New Yorker you didn't go to the old Times Square and you don't go to the new one. It's a non-issue.

My life was a sheltered one in the safe confines of the Upper East Side. As with many horror films there were four principal guidelines to ensure you didn't wind up dead before your tenth birthday:

1. DON'T GO ABOVE 96TH STREET
2. DON'T RIDE THE SUBWAYS
3. DON'T GO IN CENTRAL PARK AT NIGHT
4. DON'T WEAR AIR JORDANS

At the time, everyone in my fifth-grade homeroom had heard of someone who knew someone who had been stabbed for a pair of sneakers. You couldn't last a day on the streets of the city wearing those red, white, and black symbols of indescribable status. Nor did I want to. I didn't really follow sports, I preferred spending my allowance on deceptively-drafted Columbia House record contracts, and my mother would never spend that much money on any article of clothing (all my Ralph Lauren shirts, Brooks Brothers blazers, and fine Italian cashmere sweaters were hand-me-downs from either my older cousin Halley or Andrew Arias, a family friend my age whose growth spurt had begun at the tender age of five).

Meanwhile, I began taking indoor tennis lessons up in the Bronx. I remember vividly heading to Indian Walk across from the Whitney Museum to get fitted for a pair of sneakers for the occasion. Without even knowing the nuances of various lines within each brand, my eyes went straight to the adidas. The previous year I had spent the entire summer at camp up in Maine memorizing the lyrics to The Beastie Boys' *Paul Revere*. These guys were idols to me, proof that New York Jews could be badass. They also represented

Opposite: New York City Subway, 1980s.

AND LIVED TO

TENNIS IN NEW YORK

ONE THING STAYED THE SAME   ONE THING STAYED THE SAME

how cultures and styles mixed effortlessly downtown while my cloistered universe seemed to quietly tip-toe around cultures.[2]

The salesman emerged from the stock room with my first pair of Stan Smiths. They weren't as flashy as what some of my classmates were wearing, but I also knew I wouldn't get jumped by the Decepticons, the city's most feared gang. Soon, however, practicality turned to adoration and a bond that's lasted thirty years was formed. I loved the shoes. I loved them on the court. I loved them with khakis. I loved them with jeans. I loved them on the weekends. I loved them around the house. The only place I couldn't love them was school, where I was forced into Sebago loafers and Top-Siders. That changed when I headed off to boarding school. The color changed too. From an immaculate, scrubbed white to a lazy, mud-splattered brown, to Sharpie-scrawled doodles later on.

There was something about the shoe's simplicity that spoke to me, perhaps it was even the birth of my sartorial development, a spartan sense of style and respect of classics to which I still hold true. Over the years details would change: from Vuarnet T-shirts to North Face Mountain Light jackets to APC jeans to Junya button-downs, but one thing stayed the same, my Stan Smiths.

[1] The tipping point in my family came when my father, reporting on the dangers of the New York subways for the CBS Evening News, was mugged and his watch stolen seconds before going live on the air to report about the very phenomenon.

[2] I mean this quite literally. We were bussed from my school on Park Avenue and 73rd up to Randall's Island for sports every afternoon. When the bus landed deep in Harlem and hooked a right onto 124th Street and 3rd Avenue the bus turned silent. It was actually called "Quiet Street" for reasons that no one could explain to me s a late-comer to the school, but we were forced to almost hold our breaths as we drove across to the Triboro Bridge entrance several blocks away.

Philip Andelman
Music Video Director and Photographer

TELL ABOUT IT

IF YOU HAVEN'T

I is for If You Haven't Stopped

Although by the 2000s most would have thought both Stan and his shoe had retired from the tennis court, that wasn't exactly true. Still very active in tennis as a coach, Stan asked adidas to create a new version of the shoe that was as comfortable as the original but updated with the latest innovations found on the most recent adidas tennis shoes. adidas's response was to create the Stan Smith Millennium. Although clearly inspired by the original, it was a completely redesigned version of the Stan Smith. An upper made from synthetic leather and an injected EVA midsole meant the shoe was even more comfortable and durable and it featured new details, including embossed stripes on the sides, embroidered stripe logos on the heel and vamp, and a pull-up tab at the rear for easier fitting. Still unmistakably a Stan Smith, the shoe's latest evolution meant it was once again a court contender that Stan and fans of the original could train and compete in.

Jason Coles
Author and Sneaker Enthusiast

FOR FORTY YEARS

STOPPED   PLAYING

MILLENNIUM   MILLENNIUM

Stan's children modeling the
Millennium, 2002. *Opposite:*
adidas Stan Smith Millenium,
2000.

WHY   STOP   NOW

IT ONLY TOOK

SIX-PUS HOURS

SIX-PUS HOURS

is for It Only Took Six Hours

The ball in the case represents the longest Davis Cup match of its time. Erik Van Dillen and I were playing the doubles match against Chile-Jaime Fillol and Patricio Cornejo in 1973. After losing the first two sets 9–7 and 39–37 in five hours, we were able to come back the next day and win the match. The Little Rock, Arkansas, tennis fans got into it and it was the first time I heard the Razorbacks "Wooo Pig Sooie" cheer. The first one actually scared me. I didn't know what was going on!"
– S.S.

15 MINUTES TO

6 HOURS AND

SIX-PUS HOURS   SIX-PUS HOURS

HISTORY-MAKING TENNIS BALL
Used in Doubles Match at Burns Park, North Little Rock, Arkansas during the American Zone Finals of Davis Cup between U.S. and Chile, August 3-6, 1973. Tie won by U.S. 4-1.
U.S. team — Stan Smith, Erik van Dillen   Chile team — Patricio Cornejo, Jaime Fillol
U.S. won Doubles Match 7-9, 37-39, 8-6, 6-1, 6-3. The 39-37 set took 3 hours and 45 minutes to play and the entire match lasted 6 hours and 15 minutes, making it the longest match in Davis Cup history

147

GET THE BALL

ADIDAS ORIGINALS X FARM COMPANY

148

ADIDAS ORIGINALS X FARM COMPANY

STAN   SMITH   W   "BALI"   2017

149

STAN   SMITH   W   "BALI"   2017

JUST A FEW

U.S. PRESIDENTS   U.S. PRESIDENTS

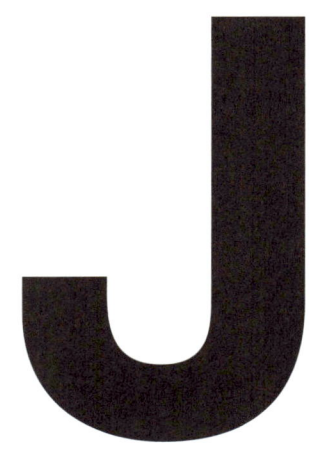

J
is for Just A Few

President Reagan held a charity event on the White House tennis court for the Nancy Reagan anti-drug campaign "Just Say No." I met Secretary of State George Shultz, who was then about sixty years old. When I saw that he was wearing my shoe, I said to him that when I had read about him and seen him on TV, that I knew that he must have quite a bit of class and wearing my shoe proved it. He said that his doctor had told him that the best tennis shoe for his particular foot problem was the Stan Smith. He suggested that adidas use his story as an endorsement of the shoe and that he should do a TV commercial for it. I liked him.

Top: Talking with President Ronald Reagan, 1981. *Bottom:* Arthur Ashe, John McEnroe, Peter Fleming, Rosie Casals, Tracey Austin, Pam Shriver, Andrea Jaeger and Marty Riessen. *Opposite:* On the White House court.

IN THE

WHITE　　　　　　　　　　SHOES

U.S.　PRESIDENTS　　　　　　　　　　U.S.　PRESIDENTS

WHITE　　　　　　　　　　HOUSE

U.S. PRESIDENTS U.S. PRESIDENTS

To Stan and Margie with best wishes, and thanks, Bill Clinton

152

Hillary and Bill Clinton visit our home, 1993.

U.S. PRESIDENTS

Over the years I met six U.S. Presidents—four of them at the White House. President Bill Clinton and Hillary along with some other dignitaries had dinner at our house during a Renaissance Weekend held at Sea Pines Resort. They said that we should come visit them at their house. I asked if they meant the "White" one. George H. W. Bush was the most active tennis player. He could slice and chop with the best of them. – S.S.

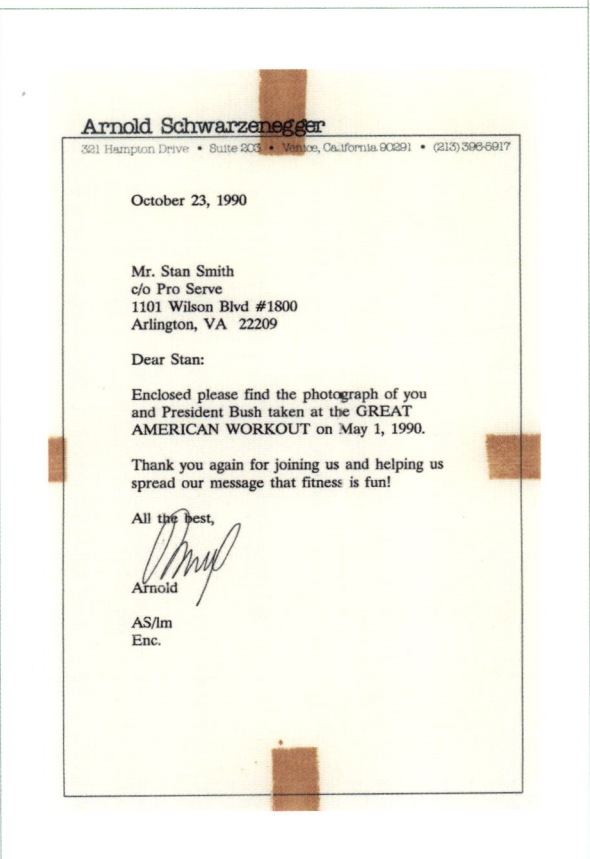

Arnold Schwarzenegger
321 Hampton Drive • Suite 203 • Venice, California 90291 • (213) 396-6917

October 23, 1990

Mr. Stan Smith
c/o Pro Serve
1101 Wilson Blvd #1800
Arlington, VA 22209

Dear Stan:

Enclosed please find the photograph of you and President Bush taken at the GREAT AMERICAN WORKOUT on May 1, 1990.

Thank you again for joining us and helping us spread our message that fitness is fun!

All the best,

Arnold

AS/lm
Enc.

Top: HW Bush demonstrating a high forehand volley on the White House court, 1991. *Bottom:* A letter from Arnold Schwarzenegger, 1990.

JEREMY TRUSTS

JEREMY   SCOTT

JEREMY   SCOTT

154

adidas x Jeremy Scott SLM
Bowling, 2012

WITH A VERY

A MAN

JEREMY   SCOTT   JEREMY   SCOTT

J

is for Jeremy Trusts

I trust in Stan Smith's shoes because the man himself has a very regal moustache and the shoe feels regal and classic to me. It's just simple, clean, and straight to the point, so it is easy to just throw on with confidence at any time with anything. The shoe is also one of the few shoes that looks and feels better the more you wear it.

Jeremy Scott
Fashion Designer

REGAL   MOUSTACHE

JOIN THE

MENTION STAN

U.S. OPEN

J
is for Join the Open Club

Winning the U.S. Open has always been the pinnacle of achievement for an American player. Until 1978, the Open was played at Forest Hills, New York, always on grass until its last three years, when the West Side Club switched to Har-Tru clay. I first played at the Open when I was seventeen and yearned to win it. I got the chance in 1971, when I played Jan Kodes, from Czechoslovakia, in the final. It was the second year of the nine-point tiebreaker format which was still a bit controversial. The semifinal was rained out on Saturday, Sunday, and Monday, so we played on Tuesday with the final on Wednesday. After winning the singles in four sets I showered, did the press interviews, got a quick bite, and went out to play the doubles final with Bob Lutz. Our opponents were the Anglo-Australian pair of Roger Taylor and John Newcombe. We got to two sets each and it was getting dark. No one wanted to stay until Thursday, so we decided to split the prize money and play a nine-point tiebreaker for the title. We ended up losing the tiebreaker and title 5–3! – S.S.

U.S. Open singles trophy, 1971.
Opposite: Not the ideal position to hit a volley in the U.S. Open.

OPEN　　　　　　　　　　　　　CLUB

U.S.　OPEN　　　　　　　　　　　　U.S.　OPEN

AT　　　　　　THE　　　　　　DOOR

ADIDAS ORIGINALS X BEDWIN & THE HEARTBREAKERS

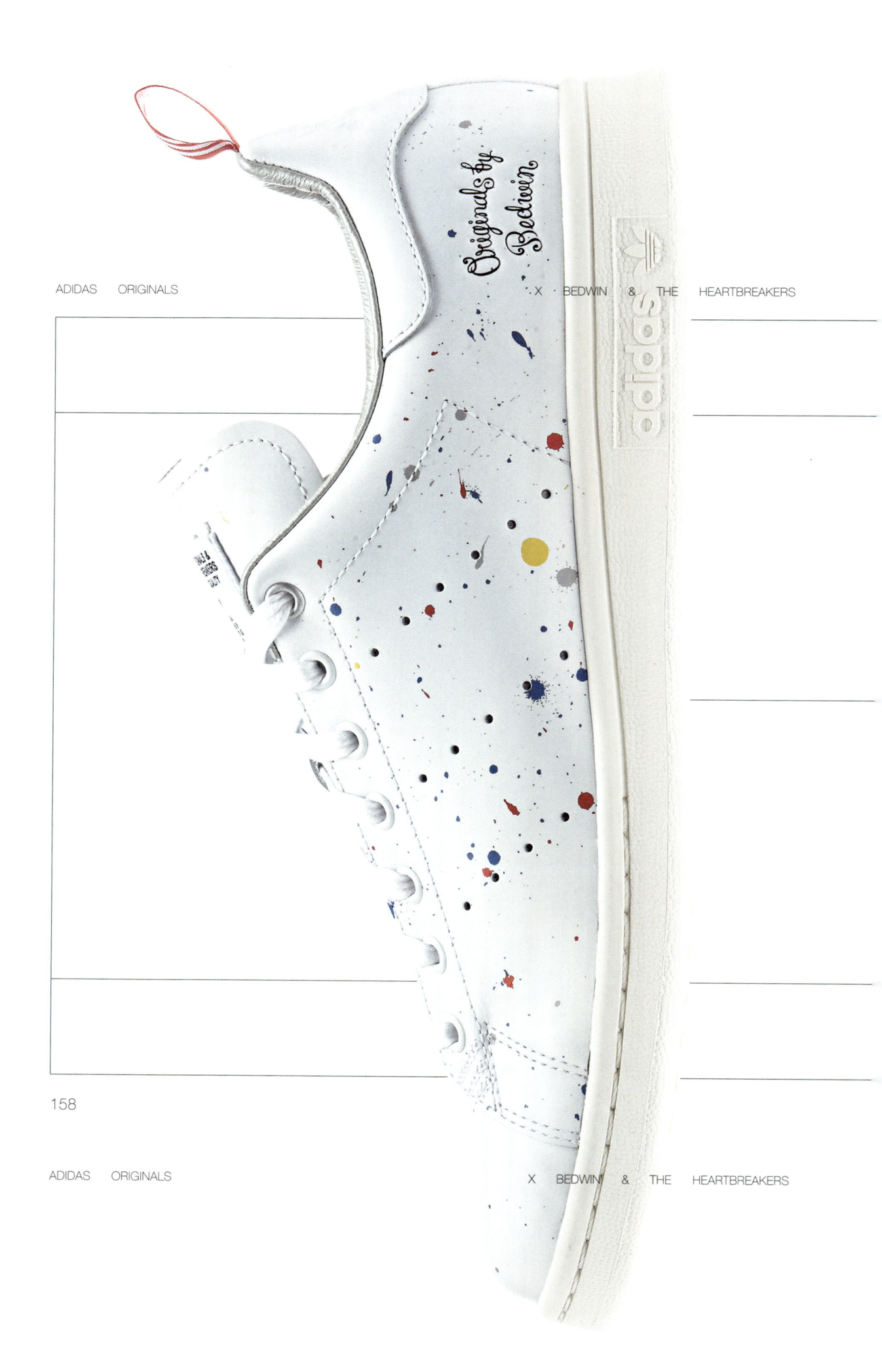

158

ADIDAS ORIGINALS X BEDWIN & THE HEARTBREAKERS

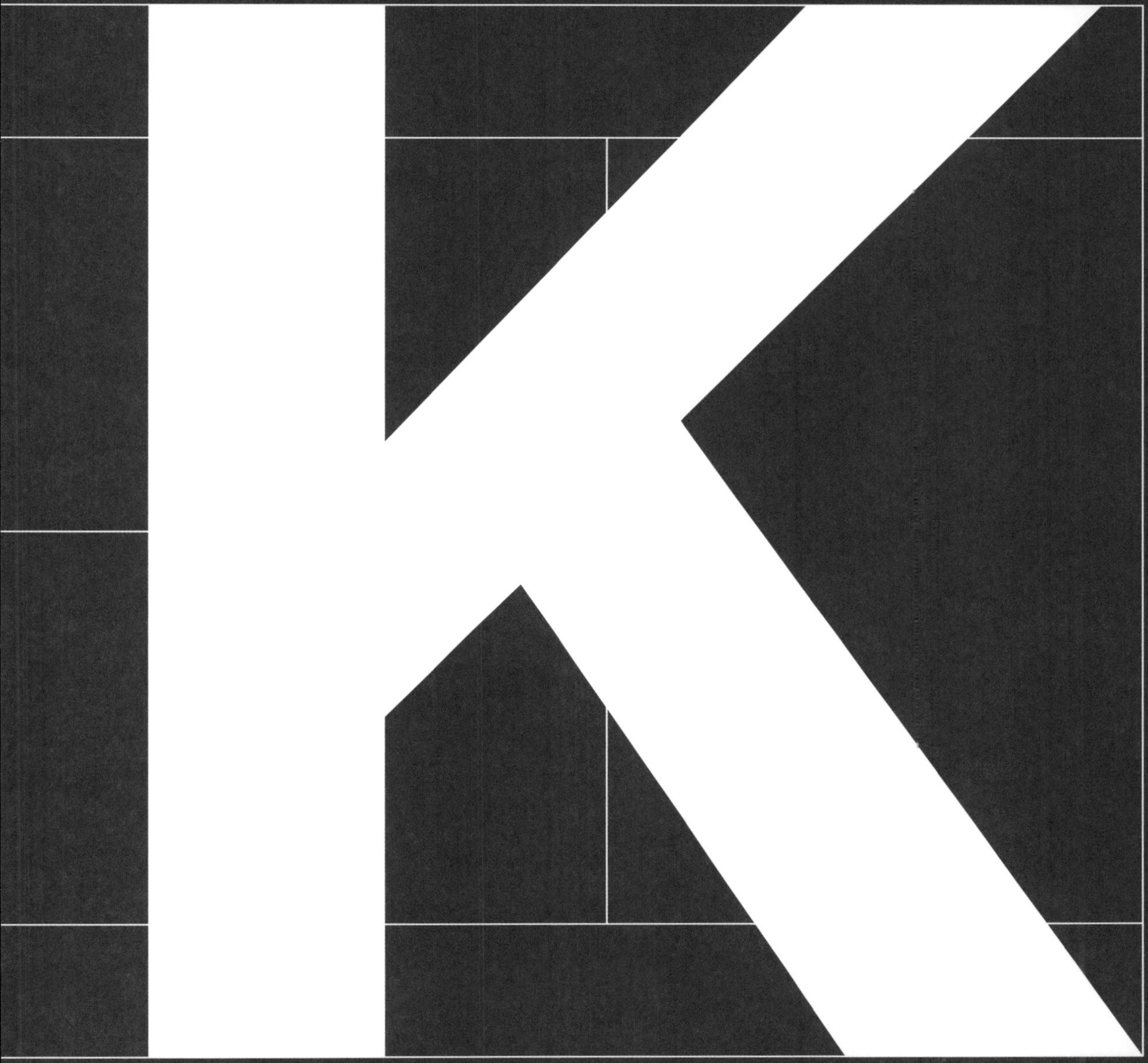

STAN SMITH 2014

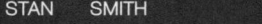

KEEPING YOUR SMITH ADDICTION

K

is for Keeping

Q: How long have you been collecting adidas sneakers for?
Chris Jack: When I started I think I was twenty, and the collection eventually grew to over 230 pairs, but since the birth of my two-year-old son, I've had to cut down a lot, purely for space in the house! My blue box stash now consists only of Stan Smiths, but I have enough to keep me going for quite a few years!

Q: Why Stan Smiths? What do they mean to you?
C.J.: For me, the simplicity and iconic look of a fresh pair of Stan Smiths just can't be beaten. Whether it be a crisp, white pair, or one of the many collaborations and colored designs that have been released recently, the quality always shines through and you'll never be disappointed by its performance and versatility. That's why it's such a classic sneaker, and why so many people wear them.

Q: Can you remember the first pair you had? Tell me a little about this.
C.J.: My first pair of Stan Smiths were the Stan Smith II, this was before I became an avid collector, and I totally ran them into the ground. They were my everyday shoe that battled all kinds of weather and terrain. So, when the reissue came about I was all over it, and from there I've became a very dedicated fan.

Q: What are the most special pair you have and why?
C.J.: I've owned many great sneakers since I began collecting, but without a doubt my most treasured pair have to be my Stan Smiths that have been customized as a dedication to my son, which were designed by Benji Blunt. We also used Stan Smiths to announce the pregnancy, so it's seemed fitting to have his own pair created.

Q: Where's the furthest place you have bought a pair from?
C.J.: I've spent many nights searching for sneakers on eBay and various sneaker forums, and often left

HEALTHY STAN

COLLECTING

Q: Why collecting sneakers, what do you think made you start?

C.J.: A huge factor in this for me comes from going to soccer games, and the terrace culture that I have been among. I remember buying the 2008 London and Stockholm sneakers, they were the two pairs that really got me hooked, and I never looked back. It became part of everyday life, from buying a new pair for a big soccer game, to queuing up outside shops in the early hours just to be in with a chance of getting a new release. It can seriously take over your life.

Q: Do you find yourself judging people now by the sneakers they are wearing?

C.J.: I would definitely say one of the first things I notice about people is what's on their feet, but there are so many trends and styles out there nowadays that I couldn't judge somebody else for their choices. Sneakers are a healthy addiction, and it's such a huge industry that so many people are involved in their own fashions; it's diversity at its best.

disappointed at how few size 12 sneakers on my want list rarely come up for sale. I once found a pair of All Odds for sale in Australia, which I absolutely adored, and they were well worth the high postage costs!

Chris Jack
Electrical Assistant
Northallerton, UK

VERY SATISFIED

KIND **OF** **A**

CENTENARY   PLATE   CENTENARY   PLATE

AN **EVEN**

BIG DEAL AND

CENTENARY PLATE   CENTENARY PLATE

K

is for Kind of a Big Deal

The beautiful Centenary plate was given to each of the past Wimbledon champions during the Centenary celebration. It is one of the few times that players have been paraded on the Centre Court and the group was the who's who of the time, including Don Budge, Fred Perry, Jack Kramer, Rod Laver, Renee Lacoste, Billie Jean King, Chrissie Evert, and Evonne Goolagong. The Duke and Duchess of Kent presided over the celebrations and Margie and I became good friends of the royal couple, and we have been invited to take tea with them in the true British tradition virtually every year since. – S.S.

The Duke and Duchess of Kent with past Wimbledon champions in the Centenary Celebration, 1977. *Opposite:* Wimbledon Centenary plate.

163

BIGGER PLATE

KEEP   FRIENDS

JEANNE   MOUTOUSSAMY-ASHE   JEANNE   MOUTOUSSAMY-ASHE

K

When I was a little girl, the classic shoe was a "Mary Jane" in black patent leather; in fact I kept a pair from when I was one year old. My mother had saved it because it was my favorite shoe. A classic shoe is also the tale of the Stan Smith shoe: a shoe for the ages.

<u>Keep Friends Close</u>

One day I was walking down Fifth Avenue between Fifty-Seventh and Fifty-Sixth Streets. As a photographer, I do not generally walk down the street with my eyes to the ground; in fact, I am most often watching everything around me. But that day the shoe for some reason caught my eye. Then I thought to look around me as I walked down that one side of the street on 5th Ave to see if there were others wearing Stan Smith sneakers. I was gobsmacked! I counted five (five!) people in Stan Smith shoes on that one block, on that one day, on an NYC street.

Jeanne Moutoussamy-Ashe
Family Friend

AND   THEY

CLOSE   ENOUGH

JEANNE   MOUTOUSSAMY-ASHE   JEANNE   MOUTOUSSAMY-ASHE

> **JEANNE MOUTOUSSAMY-ASHE**
> 360 EAST 88TH STREET #37B
> NEW YORK, NEW YORK 10128
>
> 12/14/96
>
> Dear Stan,
>
> Happy nifty-fifty!!! Congratulations — not just on turning 50 but on being who and what you are — an incredibly wonderful person/husband/father/son/friend... Please know that while you celebrate your 50th year, this family will always celebrate what you have meant to us and given to us through your friendship for so many years. You are a very special human being, Stan and we will always cherish the bond in our family friendship. There is no greater gift in life.
>
> Happy birthday — with our love, our appreciation and some very big hugs.
>
> Jeanne and Camera

CAMERA AND ARTHUR, 1992 ON THE 16th HOLE OF THE SLEEPY HOLLOW COUNTRY CLUB GOLF COURSE, NEW YORK.

Personal letter from Jeanne Moutoussamy-Ashe to Stan Smith, 1996.

BECOME   FAMILY

ADIDAS

166

ADIDAS

X   THE   HUNDREDS   STAN   SMITH   VULC   2015

167

X   THE   HUNDREDS   STAN   SMITH   VULC   2015

LESS IS

MASAAKI HOMMA

L
is for Less is More

In middle school I remember days when I was jealous of the seniors, who were wearing Stan Smiths. It is simple and stylish in a way that makes it the ultimate sneaker. Less is more. My ideal is to make clothes that are like Stan Smiths.

Masaaki Homma
Mastermind

adidas Consortium x Mastermind
Japan Stan Smith, 2014

MORE IS

MORE   **WHEN**

MASAAKI HOMMA   MASAAKI HOMMA

NOT   **BEST**

LITTLE STAN

YOUNG STAN   YOUNG STAN

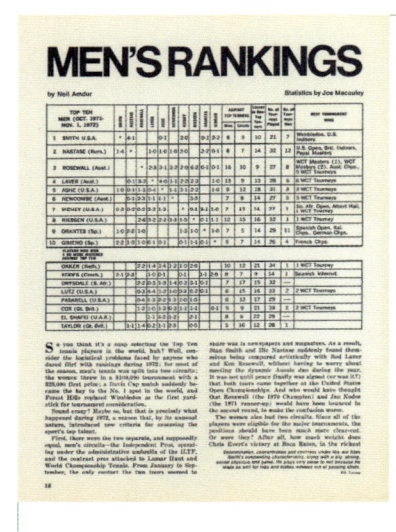

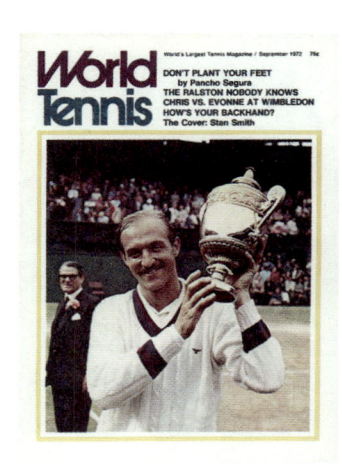

170

BIG SHOES

HAD SOME

YOUNG STAN   YOUNG STAN

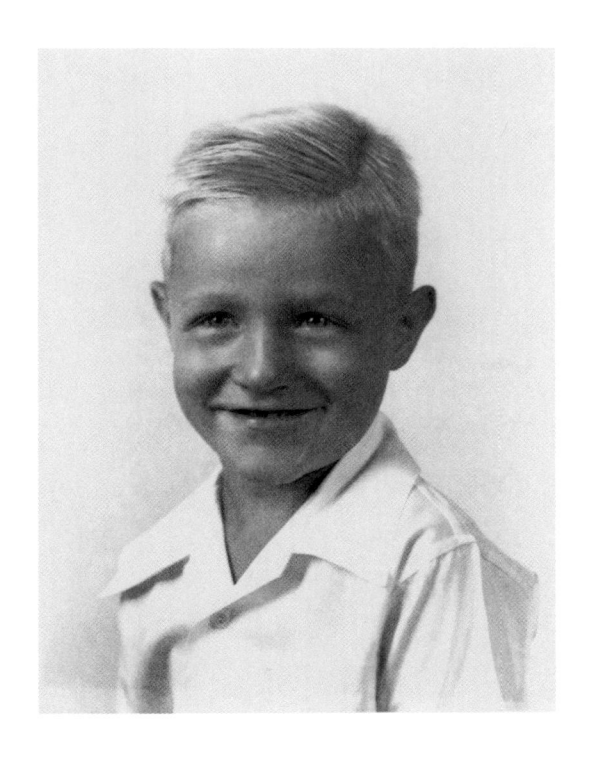

L

is for Little Stan

From an early age, I developed very specific goals. When I was sixteen, I decided I wanted to be a tennis player and listed four prime targets:

1. Become a member of the U.S. Davis Cup team.
2. Become No. 1 player in the U.S.
3. Win Wimbledon.
4. Become No. 1 in the world.

I was deliberately setting the bar high. It motivated me, made me work harder. – S.S.

Me at 7 years old. *Opposite:* Attaining my four goals.

TO FILL

YOUNG STAN

Pasadena High School Tennis Team, 1964.

YOUNG STAN

LAVER IS

SHANE BATTIER

L

is for Laver

So, who wears Rod Lavers to Stan Smith's son's wedding? Probably a dumb question. Unfortunately, I did. Not my best moment of self-awareness. My close friends Kathy Sell and Ramsey Smith were getting married at beautiful Hilton Head and, being the super tennis couple they are, decided to hold a one-point tennis tournament the day before the wedding. I was a humble basketball player, not a tennis player (although I dare you, at 6'8", to try to hit a passing shot past me when I'm at the net). The only pair of tennis shoes I had in the house belonged to Stan's longtime rival Rod Laver. Apparently, judging by the horrific looks I received

SHANE BATTIER

when I showed up at the courts wearing them, I had committed a huge faux pas.

Needless to say, I was educated very quickly on my folly (almost as fast as I was dismissed from the one-point tournament) and I slunk off the court embarrassed that I had offended the host on his home court.

It took a giant of a man to turn my fashion misstep into a good laugh. Luckily Stan Smith is a giant, not only in tennis but in life as well. He called me up to the dance floor as he was giving his wedding toast and presented me with a "special spirit award," a pair of signed Stan Smiths. How awesome is that? I still have those shoes all these years later. Thanks for saving me Stan. What a legend!

Shane Battier
Basketball champion

BE CONFUSED

NOT TO

SHANE   BATTIER   SHANE   BATTIER

"Presenting Shane Battier with my shoes at Ramsey and Kathy's wedding, 2010." – S.S.

WITH   SMITH

ADIDAS STAN SMITH

176

ADIDAS STAN SMITH

ORIGINALS   X   KZK   STAN   SMITH   84-LAB   2015

ORIGINALS   X   KZK   STAN   SMITH   84-LAB   2015

MOUSTACHE

M
is for Moustache

The Stan Smith tongue logo that has appeared on the shoe for much of its life is one of the most recognized icons in sneaker culture and fashion. But most fans don't realize it's missing something! The photograph it is based on was taken at the only time during his playing career that Stan wasn't sporting his famous moustache, and so incredibly it never made it onto the tongue logo. After many years of absence, Stan's moustache finally appeared for the Stan Smith Skateboarding version of the shoe, where a new logo was designed for the tongue, complete with a smiling Stan finally reunited with his moustache.

Jason Coles

"adidas photographed me after I shaved off my moustache. They used the photo and the 'one S' autograph for the shoe. It is still used on the classic shoes." – S.S.

LIFELONG

FREE		WEEK
MOUSTACHE		MOUSTACHE

| FACE | | LIFT |

MEDAL UP

MEDALS MEDALS

M
is for Medal

These medals represent some special tournaments, several great matches, and many fond memories of my career. The experiences were worth even more than the medals. – S.S.

1. Wimbledon Championships
S.R Smith, R.C. Lutz
Gentlemen's Doubles Runners-Up
1981

2. Copa Davis
Argentina
U.S.A.
1979

3. Wimbledon Championships
Gents Singles
Semi-Finalists
S.R. Smith
1974

4. Davis Cup
US-Czech
July 10-12, 1981

5. The Games Of
The XXVII Olympiad
Sydney 2000

6. Wimbledon Championships
1972
Mens Doubles
Runners-Up
S.R. Smith and
E.J. Van Dillen

7. 1973 WCT Finalist

8. National Collegiate Tennis Championship

9. 1974 WCT Finalist

10. Wimbledon Championships
Mens Doubles
Semi-Finalists
S.R Smith, R.C. Lutz
1976

11. Richard Milhous Nixon, 37th President of the United States of America
Inaugurated January 20th 1969

12. Wimbledon Championships
Gentlemen's Doubles Runners-Up
S.R. Smith, R.C. Lutz
1980

13. Federation Francaise De Lawn Tennis
Internationaux De France
Roland Garros
Finaliste, Double Messieurs

14. 100 Years Of Davis Cup
Tennis Australia
Australia V France
Nice
3-5 December 1999
Centenary Final

15. Stan Smith
Trophee
1972

16. Wimbledon Championships
Gents Doubles
Runners-Up
S.R. Smith,
R.C. Lutz
1974

17. International Tennis Hall of Fame
The Casino
Newport,
Rhode Island

18. Wimbledon Championships
Mens Singles
Runner-Up
S.R. Smith
1971

EXPERIENCE IN

ON   DISPLAY

MEDALS   MEDALS

1.
2.
3.
4.
5.
6.
7.
8.
9.
10.
11.
12.
13.
14.
15.
16.
17.
18.

181

YOUR   POCKETS

MARTINA JUST

MARTINA   NAVRATILOVA   MARTINA   NAVRATILOVA

182 Czechoslovak tennis player Martina Navratilova, 1978. *Opposite:* adidas Stan Smith, White/Green 2014.

AND BOUGHT 4

WENT OUT

MARTINA   NAVRATILOVA   MARTINA   NAVRATILOVA

M

is for Martina

I just went out and bought myself four pairs last week! I travel in them, I wear them practically every day, they are good for everything. I wore them on court when I first came to America, too. adidas wouldn't pay me to wear them in those days even though I had already started to win a bit, but they were the best shoe out there.

Martina Navratilova
Tennis champion

PAIRS LAST WEEK

MATERIALS OF

MATERIALS

MATERIALS

M

is for Materials

I love the different materials of the shoe. The Nubuck was the first variation and now we have some crazy different leathers—cracked, ostrich texture, reptilian à la python, pebble phoenix. Add to that cloth, canvas, primeknit, boost soles, and even wools and horsehair. The skateboard Vulc was a sturdier material and even added a fuzzy moustache. Velcro has been popular for kids and even adults. There seems to be something for every season, reason and outfit. – S.S.

adidas Scarpe Stan Smith White/Green, 2016

adidas Stan Smith Core Black, 2017

adidas Stan Smith Mesh, White Multi, 2017

EVERY PAIR OF

ANY KIND FOR

MATERIALS MATERIALS

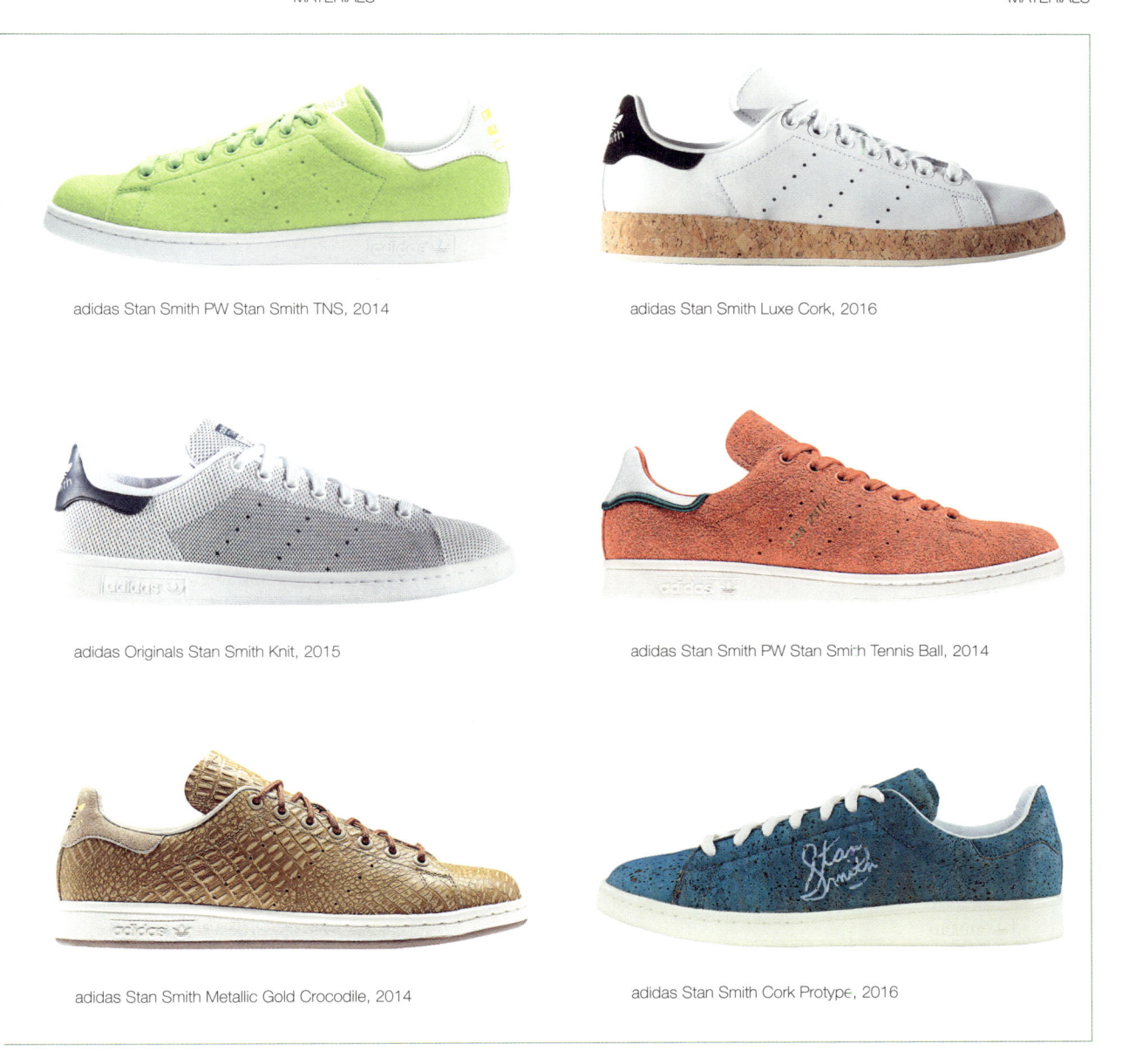

adidas Stan Smith PW Stan Smith TNS, 2014

adidas Stan Smith Luxe Cork, 2016

adidas Originals Stan Smith Knit, 2015

adidas Stan Smith PW Stan Smith Tennis Ball, 2014

adidas Stan Smith Metallic Gold Crocodile, 2014

adidas Stan Smith Cork Protype, 2016

STANS YOU FIND

ADIDAS SKATEBOARDING

186

ADIDAS SKATEBOARDING

STAN   SMITH   X   MARK   GONZALES   2007

STAN   SMITH   X   MARK   GONZALES   2007

NEWPORT IS NOT

INTERNATIONAL TENNIS HALL OF FAME　　　　　　　　　INTERNATIONAL TENNIS HALL OF FAME

188

BUT THE

JUST   ANY   HALL

INTERNATIONAL TENNIS HALL OF FAME

N

is for Newport

This was a special day because of the honor for me and my fellow inductees, and it was made all the more special with my family being there to witness the event. Now that I am president of the International Tennis Hall of Fame I get an insider's look at just how difficult it is to get nominated, and then actually elected, into the Hall. The Nominating Committee, consisting of some twenty ex-players and media experts, have an intense and detailed meeting at Wimbledon every year, analyzing every aspect of an applicant's career and character. Now I am even more aware that those who do make it through the process are truly the best who have ever played the game. – S.S.

ITHF medal presented to all inductees. *Opposite:* My son Ramsey with me at my induction into the International Tennis Hall of Fame, 1987.

BIG   ONE

NEVER FORGET A

VIJAY AMRITRAJ

N
is for Never Forget

Stan and I have some very interesting things in common. Besides being born on the same day a few years apart, we have played against each other and together while strangely being unbeaten! But the Stan Smith shoe—which I have always thought of as classy, elegant, sporty, and casual all at the same time—is the shoe that the kids love without knowing that Stan Smith was an actual person! That just shows the amazing quality of the shoe. It looks and feels exactly like the man: historic and modern, never going out of fashion. But another connection is that the shoe is made in my hometown of Chennai, India. Just brilliant.

Vijay Amritraj
Tennis champion

WHEN IT'S THE

FRIEND'S BIRTHDAY

VIJAY AMRITRAJ   VIJAY AMRITRAJ

"An opponent, partner, and friend." – S.S.   191

SAME AS YOURS

NASTASE WELCOMES

ILIE   NASTASE   ILIE   NASTASE

192

TO THE SCENE

STAN SMITH BACK

ILIE NASTASE   ILIE NASTASE

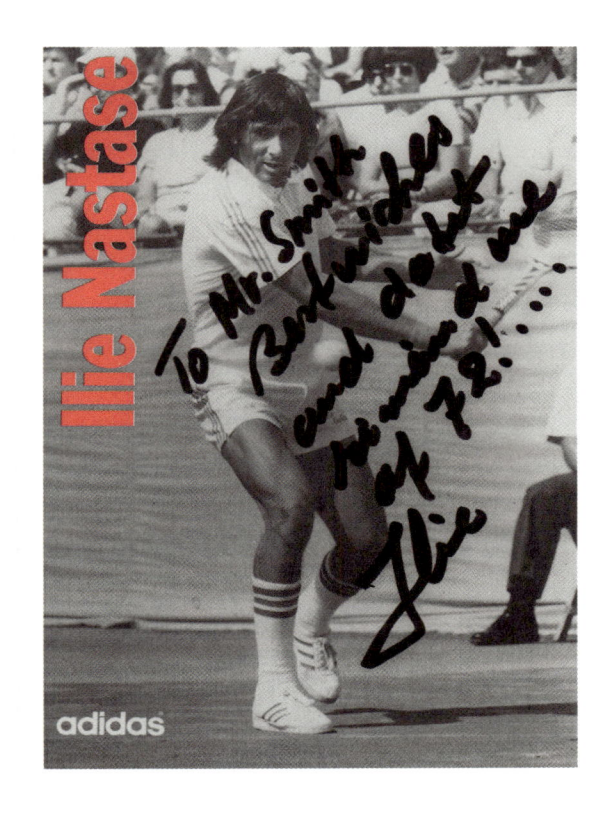

N

is for Nastase

Despite all that had happened, someone in Bucharest dreamt up the strange idea of celebrating our 1972 victory by inviting us back for the thirtieth anniversary in 2002. I didn't want to go at first but was eventually persuaded, and Tom Gorman and I went back to the scene of the crime! I played a set against Ilie Nastase, but the highlight came when Tom and I changed partners at 3–all and I played with Tiriac! It was all very lighthearted and a little surreal. Tiriac was playing in a pair of long trousers and he looked like Don Budge. "I can't believe you came," he said. "Neither can I," I replied. – S.S.

"To Mr. Smith Best wishes and don't remind me of '72!... Ilie" *Opposite:* adidas catalogue 'The Complete Tennis Line', 1974.

OF THE CRIME

ADIDAS SMITH

194

ADIDAS SMITH

ORIGINALS   X   WINGS   AND   HORNS   2015

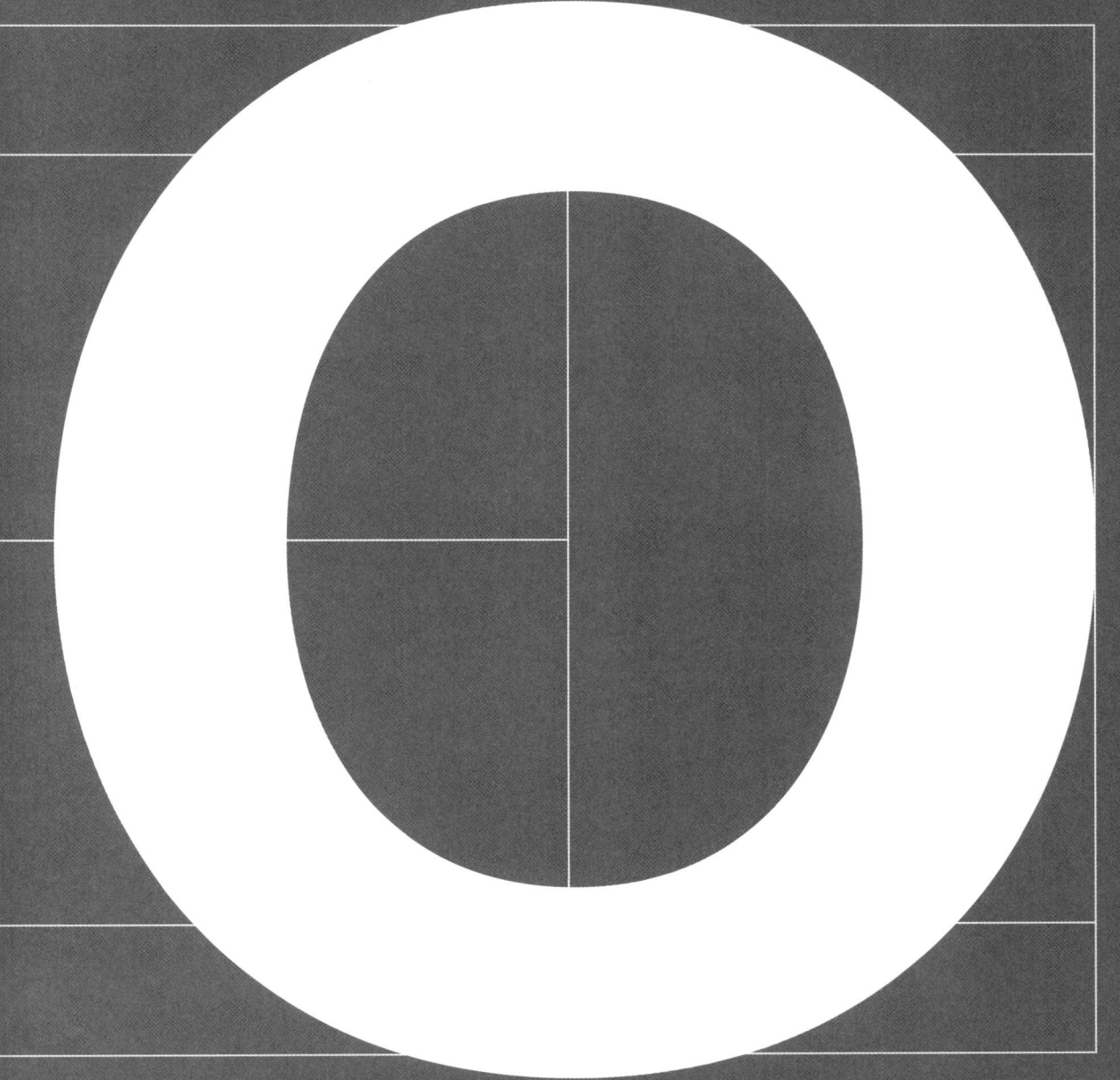

195

ORIGINALS   X   WINGS   AND   HORNS   2015

OBVIOUSLY THERE

USC TROJANS

O

is for Obviously

I was lucky, upon entering USC at the age of seventeen, to come under the influence of the head tennis coach, George Toley. You only have to look at the list of players he coached to realize how good he was. Rafael Osuna, Alex Olmedo, Dennis Ralston, Raul Ramirez, Bob Lutz—he turned all of them into Grand Slam champions in singles or doubles. As well as me! There were some other great coaches, especially in California, but for me, George was the best. – S.S.

IN THOSE USC

WAS   SOMETHING

USC   TROJANS   USC   TROJANS

Clockwise from top left: Alex Olmedo, Dennis Ralston, Raul Ramirez, Rafael Osuna, Bob Lutz, and Stan Smith.

WATER   FOUNTAINS

ONE MAGICAL

KAREN VAN GODTSENHOVEN

O
is for One Magical Sneaker

In the Stan Smith shoe, we find a perfect blend of functionality and design, the linear perforations giving the shoe its distinct design as well as ventilation for the foot.

Because of this discrete and minimalist unisex design, the shoe has become a staple for people working in the arts and creative fields: it is like a secret code that entails that one appreciates good design. Not showy, it is an understated design piece that nevertheless also has a wide, democratic appeal because it is a classic item that can be combined with both casual as well as formal outfits.

KAREN VAN GODTSENHOVEN

The magic of the Stan Smith shoe is that it can pass as a normal sneaker but also be used as a dressed-up shoe to a black-tie event.

Because the name of the shoe is not a brand or a designer, the name of Stan Smith has gotten more anonymous; it has detached itself from the person and has become a type, much like Doc Martens have come to mean the type of boots or Chucks have come to mean the type of sneakers.

Karen Van Godtsenhoven
Associate Curator, The Costume Institute,
The Metropolitan Museum of Art

EVERY HOUR

SNEAKER FOR OF THE DAY

KAREN VAN GODTSENHOVEN

Deconstructed Stan Smith shoe, 2013.

ONLY ONE

SO MANY

STAN   FANS

STAN   FANS

O

is for Only One Shoe

"I've been wearing Stan Smiths since junior high school, and glad you can still get them! I remember a panic a little while ago when there was a rumor around that they were going to stop making them. Now you see them everywhere, but they're still a beloved classic."

"They look even better beaten up."

Sofia Coppola
Artist and Director, New York, USA

Pierre Elma
Videographer, Hong Kong

200

adidas Stan Smith, Core black/Green, 2017

SHOE　　　　　　　　　　　　　　　　　　　　　　　　　HAS

STAN　FANS　　　　　　　　　　　　　　　　　STAN　FANS

"I bought my Stans with my Dad and we actually got the same pair. It makes me smile to think that we're twinning!"

"I am the kind of person that, even at work, likes things to be extremely simple, especially things that I wear. In this world, there are many simple things, but something that is universal and doesn't just fit during a certain trend, a shoe with such a pure design without vanity—simply pursuing the greatest functionality, that is what's most important, I think."

Tsuyoshi Nimura
Fashion Director and Stylist, Tokyo, Japan

Martina Cortese
Student, Rome, Italy

adidas Stan Smith, White/Blue, 2017　　　　adidas Stan Smith, Green Suede, 2014　　　201

DIFFERENT　　　　　　　　　　　　　　　　　　　LIVES

ADIDAS — CONSORTIUM

X   ALIFE   X   STARCOW   STAN   SMITH   2017

X   ALIFE   X   STARCOW   STAN   SMITH   2017

PÉLE CROSSED

PÉLE PÉLE

P

is for Péle

"While traveling the world playing football, I crossed paths with tennis legend Stan Smith. Through the years, his passion, talent, and dedication to the sport of tennis created a legacy that still inspires the younger generation on the court and in life."

Péle
Soccer champion

Opposite: "Jeff Borowiak, Arthur Ashe, Pele, and Tom Okker in Lagos in 1976 for a tournament. We fled the country when the President of Nigeria was murdered." – S.S.

STAN CROSSED

STAN'S   PATH

PÉLE   PÉLE

PELE'S   PATH

PARTNERS IN

BOB LUTZ

BOB LUTZ

U.S.L.T.A.
UNITED STATES OPEN TENNIS CHAMPIONSHIP
MEN'S DOUBLES
1968
WON BY

GREAT FRIENDS

CRIME   REMAIN

BOB   LUTZ   BOB   LUTZ

P
is for Partners

I don't know why our names are not on the plate, but I do know that the years have gone by fast and this year Bob Lutz and I will be celebrating our fiftieth anniversary of winning the first U.S. Open doubles title and, of course, the anniversary of our good friend Arthur Ashe winning the first singles. The Open has a very special place in my heart and Bob was always special to me in my career. Technically we were a perfect fit with Bob so consistent on the left side and me being more aggressive in the right court. We had different personalities, but Bob was always easy to get along with. – S.S.

Bob Lutz and me, 1980. *Opposite:* This is a mystery trophy—for some reason our names were not engraved on it.

FOR   LIFE

PUT A RING

RINGS

P is for Put a Ring on It

When a player is inducted into the International Tennis Hall of Fame at Newport, Rhode Island, he or she is presented with a plaque and certificate to commemorate one of the greatest moments in a tennis player's life. But that is not all. A few years later, inductees are invited to attend a tournament where they enjoyed particular success and, during an on-court ceremony, they are presented with an IHoF ring—once again recognizing their accomplishments.

RINGS

During my time at USC, I won the NCAA singles title once and the doubles title twice. Many years later the current USC tennis coach, Peter Smith, was involved in creating rings for all the great USC athletes and I was among the first class to be inducted in 1994. There were fifteen of us—including O. J. Simpson! So, I added another ring to my collection. A few years later, when I was coach of the U.S. Olympic tennis team in 2000, I received another.

WCT Champion ring. *Opposite (clockwise from top):* USC National Champion ring, ITHF ring, Fellow Hall of Fame inductee Alex Olmedo and me with our ITHF rings.

I KNOW

ON IT SO

RINGS   RINGS

Lamar Hunt, the great sports ertrepreneur who owned the Kansas City Chiefs, created World Championship Tennis in 1970. The CEO Mike Davies divided the world's top players into three travelling groups—Red, Green, and Blue—and sent them off on a ten-tournament global tour. The top eight finishers qualified for the WCT finals in Dallas, which for years was considered one of the world's best showcases for the game. Drawing on his football experience, Lamar had a WCT ring designed for the champion. I was lucky enough to win one in 1973, the year I beat Arthur Ashe in the final. – S.S.

IT'S REAL

ADIDAS ORIGINALS X KVADRAT

210

ADIDAS ORIGINALS X KVADRAT

STAN   SMITH   2017

Q

211

STAN   SMITH   2017

QUALITY ON

SKATEBOARDING

Q

is for Quantity

Although it began life as a tennis shoe, you may not realize that the Stan Smith has always been popular in other sports. It's a little-known fact that you can play a pretty decent game of basketball in them! However, one of its more unexpected fanbases has grown among some of the most sneaker-savvy competitors in any sport: skateboarders. A long bone of contention between them has been the virtues of vulcanized soles versus cup soles. The Stan Smith became a firm favorite with the cup fans because its cup sole design provided all the comfort and stability they loved, but meant that "Vulc" fans, who prefer the better board feel

SKATEBOARDING

that thinner vulcanized soles give them, could only look on in envy. But that all changed when adidas Skateboarding announced a Stan Smith design just for skaters. The brand-new shoe had all the comfort of the Stan Smith, but with a vulcanized sole and a vectorized traction pattern designed specially for skating. The shoe that gave the Vulc fans the ride they craved, but with the smooth ride and support that cup fans loved.

Jason Coles

NO MATTER

THE COURT

SKATEBOARDING   SKATEBOARDING

Film stills from adidas Skateboarding
The Legend of Stan Smith, 2014.
Opposite: adidas Stan Smith Vulc,
White/Black, 2015.

THE SPORT

QUOTE ME

STAN FANS

Q

is for Quote Me

"I remember wearing Stan Smith shoes all the time when I was young. I wore them to school. I wore them to church. I wore them to play football. I still wear them to this day, and so does my wife, daughters, and son. These shoes have become family members in the Villa household!"

David Villa
Soccer champion, New York, USA

STAN FANS

"When I was around twelve, my mom went to Shanghai for work for quite a long time and I was quite pissed at her for not being around. When she came back home, she brought me a pair of white sports shoes as a gift. I didn't know that much about the shoes at that time, but later in school my best friend told me they were Stan Smiths. The boys went wild, and of course I got a lot of attention for them. I did have a great time. I moved to Shanghai as a tattoo artist, with my new pairs of Stan Smiths. I still feel as proud wearing them as when I was a kid."

Qiang Wenwen
Tattoo Artist, Shanghai, China

adidas Stan Smith Suede Blue, 2014

AND REMEMBER TO

ON THAT

STAN FANS · STAN FANS

"All I know about Stan Smith is that he plays tennis. I got them before sixth grade. My mom got them for me because I needed new shoes. I like them because they are comfortable and they go with everything. My first pair started getting threadbare and too small, so I decided since I was done with them my friends could all sign them. When my second pair, the ones I wear now, got a little dirty I did the same thing. I wear the shoes every day to school and pretty much everywhere."

Olivia Silva
Student, Miami, USA

"In 2015 I saw John Legend in a restaurant in Leça da Palmeira, before he got on stage at the MEO Mares Vivas festival. We didn't have a conversation, but he had the chance to tell me that my Stan Smiths were awesome!"

Jorge Santos
Soccer champion, Porto, Portugal

adidas Stan Smith zig zag, White/Green, 2015

MENTION THE SHOE

ADIDAS X STAN SMITH

216

ADIDAS X STAN SMITH

ORIGINALS   FIVE-TWO   3   PROJECT   X   MAHARISHI   2009

217

ORIGINALS   FIVE-TWO   3   PROJECT   X   MAHARISHI   2009

RULES OF STYLE

NIC GALWAY

R is for Rules

"The difference between and old pair of sneakers and an old pair of Stan Smith sneakers is that the Stan Smiths are an icon," says Nic Galway, Global Designer at adidas. "He may not have realized it at the time, but Stan was part of a pioneering product. The shoe was the latest innovation of its time, a design for the highest level of sporting competition. As sneaker culture evolved into a wider story, it came to have its own cultural meaning. The Stan Smith was simple and honest and was worn by a Wimbledon champion. But its clean design enabled it to be adopted by anyone, anywhere for whatever purpose."

Galway, who came to adidas in the 1999 from a background of designing cars, train engines, and even harness equipment for rock climbing at Coventry in England, began working in the tennis division almost by chance and was present at the U.S. Open when Stan Smith met Pharrell Williams. "It was one of those moments when the collaborative environment we like to promote at adidas bore immediate fruit. Pharrell knew little of tennis but was so open to learning. 'I need to know more about tennis,' I remember him saying and I sat behind them as Stan patiently explained the scoring system during a match. They became fast friends almost immediately." The ability of his shoe to be a vehicle for crossing boundaries and creating new partnerships is one of the things that excites Stan most about the continuing success of a product that has transformed itself into a universal fashion item.

"Sneakers can say different things and make all kinds of statements about who you are or want to be," says Galway. "But the Stan Smith is subtler than that. Wearing them, you can be noticed or not noticed. If two people are wearing the same sneaker at a party, that might be wrong if the design was making too big a statement. But if several people are wearing the Stan Smith, there is nothing awkward about it. It's just what people are doing."

Nic Galway
SVP of Global Design, adidas Originals and Style
Interviewed by Richard Evans

RULES OF THE

CAN CHANGE BUT

NIC   GALWAY   NIC   GALWAY

GAME MUST STAY

RAF SWAPS

THREE STRIPES   ONE R

R

is for Raf

A question often asked about the Stan Smith is, "Where are the adidas Three Stripes?" The answer lies in the fact that when the shoe was first created, tennis was still very much an amateur sport. The endorsement of brands by players was strictly forbidden, and clothing had to be all white without any identifying marks. Complying with the rules meant that adidas couldn't apply their famous Three Stripes to the shoe and so a clever solution was found. In place of the stripes, three rows of perforated holes were added that appeared to be there purely for ventilation, but were also an inventive way to have "stripes" on the shoe without breaking the

adidas x Raf Simons Stan Smith, White/Green, 2014

FOR A

THREE   STRIPES

THREE   STRIPES   ONE   R

rules. The holes themselves have since become a core part of the shoe's identity, so much so that when celebrated designer Raf Simons was asked to create a signature version of the shoe—believing there was nothing he could, or even should change about the shoe's classic design—he simply rearranged the ventilation holes into an "R."

Jason Coles

SIMPLE   R

THREE STRIPES ONE R

"I have a personal connection with the Stan Smith, as it is fair to say that for ten years, from my teens well into my twenties, I didn't wear any other shoes —only Stan Smiths. It was very obvious for me to collaborate with adidas."

– Raf Simons

Raf X Stan Smith Cf, Grey/White/Pumpkin, 2014. *Opposite:* Fashion Designer/Creative Director Raf Simons, 2009.

THREE   STRIPES   ONE   R

THREE　　STRIPES　　　　　　　　　　　　　　　　　ONE　　R

224　　adidas x Raf Simons Stan Smith,　　　　　　　　adidas x Raf Simons Stan Smith,
　　　　Green, 2015.　　　　　　　　　　　　　　　　　Purple, 2015.

THREE   STRIPES   ONE   R

adidas x Raf Simons Stan Smith,
Yellow, 2015

adidas x Raf Simons Stan Smith
'Distressed Light Brown', 2015

REBELS WITH

FIGHTING FOR

ATP   BOYCOTT

R
is for Rebels

I was the Wimbledon Champion but couldn't defend my title. The 1973 boycott of the Championships was a huge, defining moment in the history of our sport and it affected all of us, but for me, personally, it was even more dramatic and painful.

I had not only won the title the year before but had continued to play the best tennis of my life in the early months of 1973, winning seven of the eleven WCT tournaments I played, beating the great Rod Laver four times in the process. I was itching to get back on Centre Court and defend my crown.

However, I was a member of the Board of Directors of the Association of Tennis Professionals, a fledgling organization that had been born, after a long and difficult pregnancy, at the U.S. Open just nine months before. It had been formed because, despite the advent of open tennis in 1968, professional players were still under the thumb of their amateur national associations.

Despite being allowed back to compete at the world's biggest championships like Wimbledon, the U.S. Open, etc., the national associations, run by part-time amateurs, still wanted to control our lives. Incredible as it may seem now, the Australian Association would not let their players leave the country until April each year, thus ensuring that they played all the local tournaments.

Inevitably, my colleagues on the ATP tour chafed against being ordered about by amateurs who were more concerned with handing over trophies on finals day and wearing the right tie and badge than worrying about the welfare of professional players.

Matters came to a head when Nikki Pilic ran into a conflict with his Yugoslav Association. They wanted him to play the Davis Cup, as he always had done in the past, but the dates clashed with the WCT World Doubles Championships for which he had qualified with the Australian Allan Stone. Pilic had a legal contract with Lamar Hunt's organization and he was not about to break it. The Yugoslav association promptly suspended him.

The funny thing was that Nikki Pilic was not the most

Opposite: Cliff Richey, Arthur Ashe, Nikki Pilic, Jack Kramer, and me debating a boycott of Wimbledon, 1973.

A CAUSE

ATP   BOYCOTT   ATP   BOYCOTT

PLAYERS'   RIGHTS

ATP   BOYCOTT   ATP   BOYCOTT

popular player in the locker room, but this was not about Pilic, it was about principle. When Cliff Drysdale, the first ATP President, and some of us board members started canvassing the opinions of our colleagues during the Italian Open, we found an air of militancy that was reaching boiling point.

A large majority of the players were saying, "Enough is enough!" They wanted a say in the affairs of their own profession, a right to have representatives at the table sharing in the decision making. It did not seem too much to ask.

However, Allan Heyman, a Danish lawyer who was president of the International Federation at the time, thought that it was. Like his colleagues, he was frightened of losing control. So, he laid out a plan which he thought would spike our guns when we threatened a boycott. He decreed that the Yugoslav ban on Pilic would last through the first week of Wimbledon. That, he felt assured, would be pushing the players' loyalty to the ATP too far.

One American official, talking to the former Wimbledon finalist Dennis Ralston, said smugly, "You guys will boycott any tournament in the world, but not Wimbledon."

That turned out to be a very bad mistake. By the time the tour had arrived in England for the pre-Wimbledon tournaments, Jack Kramer, who was our CEO, had called emergency meetings at the Westbury Hotel in Mayfair. Happily, for the future of the game, we had an exceptionally strong board made up of motivated, intelligent people who had the guts to meet a crisis head-on and stick to their principles.

Along with Drysdale, who found himself working all hours, we had Arthur Ashe, Mark Cox, the former British Davis Cup captain John Barrett, Jim McManus, Jaime Fillol, Ismail El Shafei, and myself. Although they were not on the board, we also had John Newcombe, Charlie Pasarell, Cliff Richey, and others urging us to stay united and not break ranks when the heat was turned up by the British media.

The threat of a boycott of Wimbledon became front-page news. Wimbledon was sacrosanct, so there was no question whose side the editors were going to take. The players had to be the villains, right? We were just a bunch of greedy, money-grabbing pros. The fact that it was all about a battle for control not money, got lost in the mix.

But the Fleet Street editors had a problem. They needed villains and scratched their heads when they looked at the board. Cliff, Arthur, Mark, Newk, myself, and many of the other players involved (Rod Laver, Ken Rosewall, and Roy Emerson were fully supportive, too) had become heroes with the British public over the years. How could we be branded as villains?

So, the press turned their ire on Jack Kramer, who—despite being a former Wimbledon champion himself—was viewed as a rich, cigar-chomping Yank goading

Opposite: Ilie Nastase, Tom Okker, and me with the legal team, 1973.

the naive players to harm Wimbledon. No one mentioned that Jack was working for us for free, so strongly did he believe in our cause. That didn't fit the narrative.

The way the narrative worked out, after endless meetings burning the midnight oil right up to the end of the week before Wimbledon, changed the face of professional tennis forever. After voting narrowly for a boycott, we convened a second time the next day just to make sure we had a majority, because we were all aware what a momentous decision we were about to make.

It turned out that the vote was split down the middle, leaving Drysdale to make the deciding vote. Proving himself to be a master politician, Cliff abstained, which meant that the vote of the previous evening stood. We would boycott Wimbledon.

"I was in a very difficult position, but my prime task was to keep our young association together," Drysdale explained later. "I knew if I had voted against a boycott at least half the membership would have walked out. But not everyone was convinced we were doing the right thing. So, I let matters run their course."

Despite the frustration we all felt at being denied the chance to play in the world's number-one tournament, I have never regretted the decision. It was a tipping point in the history of the game and it bonded the ATP players pretty dramatically. We realized that, if we stuck together, despite being rivals on court, we could do almost anything. It was tough to imagine doing anything more difficult than boycotting Wimbledon.

Almost ninety players withdrew on the eve of the championships, right after the draw had been made. Of course, it had to be redone, with a flood of young players who were not ATP members or representatives of Communist Eastern European countries who would have had their passports confiscated had they joined us, gaining entry. Jan Kodes, a Czech, duly became champion, beating Alex Metreveli of the Soviet Union in the final.

I was proud to be part of that board. Within months, with the help of our legal adviser Donald Dell, a Men's International Professional Tennis Council had been formed, consisting of three members of the ITF: three tournament directors and three members of the ATP. Finally, the players had a voice.

These things go in cycles. For a while many top players were not interested in becoming involved with running the game, but that has not been the case in the last decade. The Top Four of Roger Federer, Rafael Nadal, Novak Djokovic, and Andy Murray have not only dominated the men's tour to a startling degree on court, but they have proved to be leaders off it as well. All have served in various positions on the ATP Players Council and have taken decisive leadership roles in the issues of the day. It's the way it should be. – S.S.

Nikki Pilic, Cliff Drysdale, Arthur Ashe, and Jack Kramer, 1973.

232

ADIDAS

ORIGINALS

X CONCEPTS STAN SMITH 2014

233

X CONCEPTS STAN SMITH 2014

SIGN YOUR

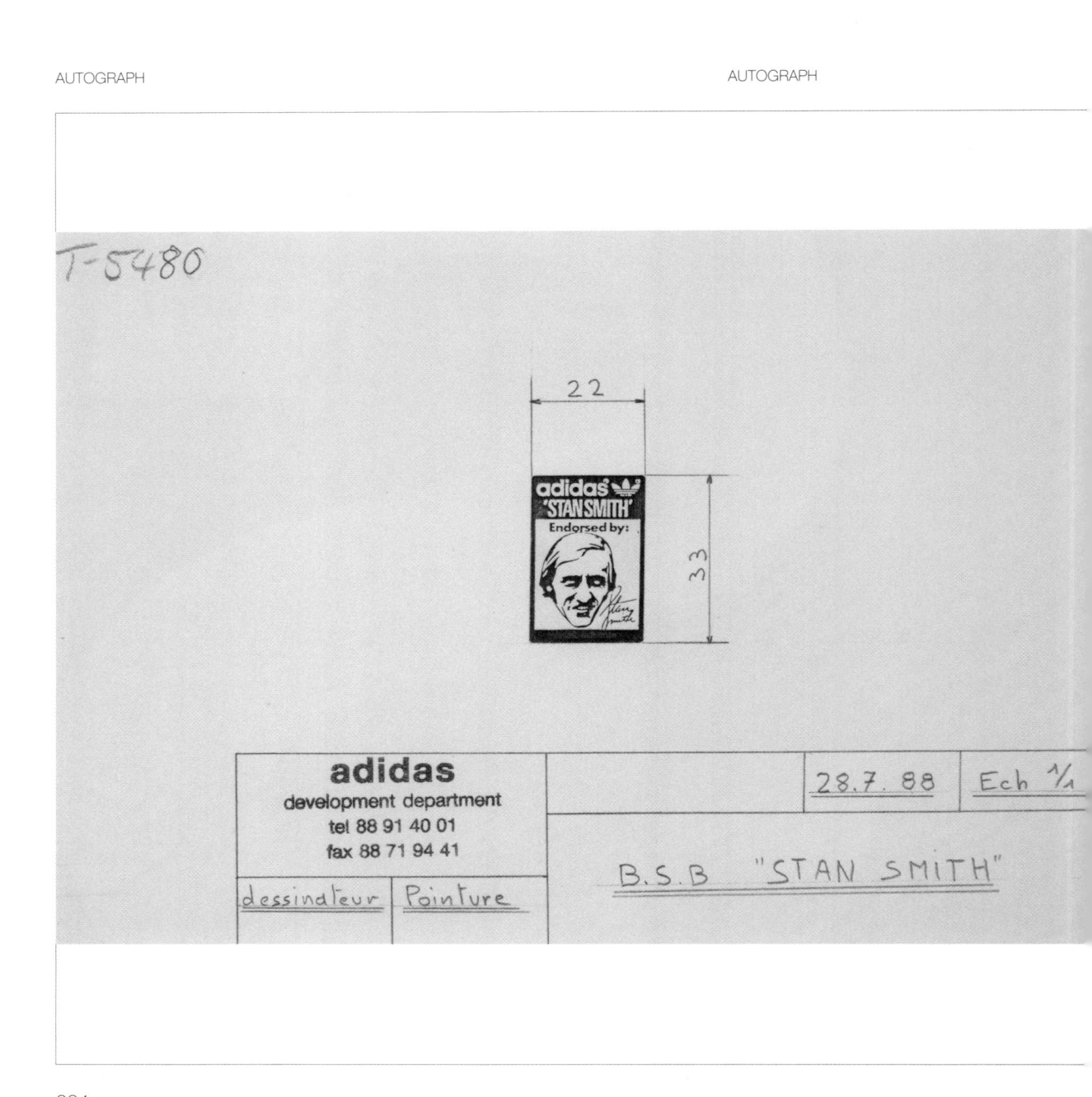

AUTOGRAPH　　　　　　　　　　　　　　　　　　　　　AUTOGRAPH

T-5480

22

33

adidas
development department
tel 88 91 40 01
fax 88 71 94 41

dessinateur | Pointure

28.7.88 | Ech 1/1

B.S.B "STAN SMITH"

ON THE

NAME RIGHT

AUTOGRAPH   AUTOGRAPH

S

is for Sign Your Name

Early in the 1970s I was doing a sporting goods store appearance in Atlanta for adidas and a young woman came in to look around. She saw me there and asked what I was doing. I don't think she was a tennis fan, but she was creative. She suggested that I use one "S" in doing autographs and put the tan after the S above the mith after the S below the tan. I stopped using that signature for several years but have gone back to it.
– S.S.

The "one S" has been on the shoe since 1973. *Opposite:* The face and autograph design for the shoe has never changed.

DOTTED LINE

SHAPE   SO

SHAPES   SHAPES

S

is for Shape

The original shoe was as simple as you can get, and it is one of the reasons it has been popular. We now have high tops, mid tops, boots, pointed toes, and even clogs. When my daughter saw the wedge she immediately had to have them. Now she is cooler and taller. – S.S.

adidas Stan Smith Slim, 2009

adidas Stan Smith Mid, White, 2017

adidas Stan Smith Clog

CAN   TAKE

SIMPLE   IT

SHAPES   SHAPES

adidas Stan Smith "Bold", 2018

adidas Stan Smith Trefoil Mid Natural Blue, 2011

Vintage adidas Lady Smith, 1987

adidas Pharrell Williams Tennis Hu Shoes, 2017

adidas adicross Classic Leather, 2018

adidas Stan Smith Up, Black, 2014

adidas Stan Smith Cutout, 2017

adidas Stan Smith Platform Sandal, 2014

adidas Stan Smith, 2005

237

MANY   FORMS

SEGURA'S SCHOOL

PANCHO SEGURA

PANCHO SEGURA

PUTS BRAIN

S

is for Segura's School

At the Pasadena Tennis Patrons, I was always learning and Pancho Segura, who came over from Beverly Hills to work with us on Saturday mornings, gave us the advantage of his brilliant tactical tennis brain. He was especially good at teaching us how to play players with different styles and how to take advantage of their weaknesses. I consider Pancho to have been one of the smartest player/coaches ever. – S.S.

From left to right: Butch Bucholtz, Pancho Segura, me, and an ATP official at Pancho's ATP Award ceremony, 1981. *Opposite:* Pancho Segura at Wimbledon, 1946.

STAND UP

PROTEST SHOE   PROTEST SHOE

S

is for Stand Up

I wish I could remember the day I wore my first pair of Stan Smith but I can't. I think I was thirteen or fourteen years old. It was summertime and I wanted to be just like every other kid in Italy. Everyone had a pair of Stan Smith in Italy in the 1990s. I loved them, all white with the green heel—I didn't take them off until the following fall. Actually, I've never really taken them off at all—after that first pair, I bought so many more. Many colors came and went over the last almost thirty years—green, blue, red—I had a pair that traveled with me almost everywhere, from the concrete jungle of New York, to the African bush, to the Polynesian sand. But somehow they didn't survive a wild trek in Iguazu… pity my poor travel companion. The pair I'm most attached to are the first ones I ever bought. I was fourteen and asked all my friends to sign them. I was in high school, in the mid-1990s, and everybody was talking about the nuclear testing in Mururoa, in the Pacific Ocean. I went with some friend to a protest march and wrote a message that said: "Stop nuclear testing in Mururoa" on the side of my Stans. After that day, the pair became a lucky charm to me. I wore them to several civil rights marches that I went to. I still love them and even if the message is almost unreadable, they remind me of these amazing moments in my life!

Giovanni Alpi
Osteopath

FEET

FROM YOUR

PROTEST   SHOE   PROTEST   SHOE

UP

ADIDAS ORIGINALS						X STAR WARS EDITION

ADIDAS ORIGINALS						X STAR WARS EDITION

STAN   SMITH   80S   "MASTER   YODA"   2011

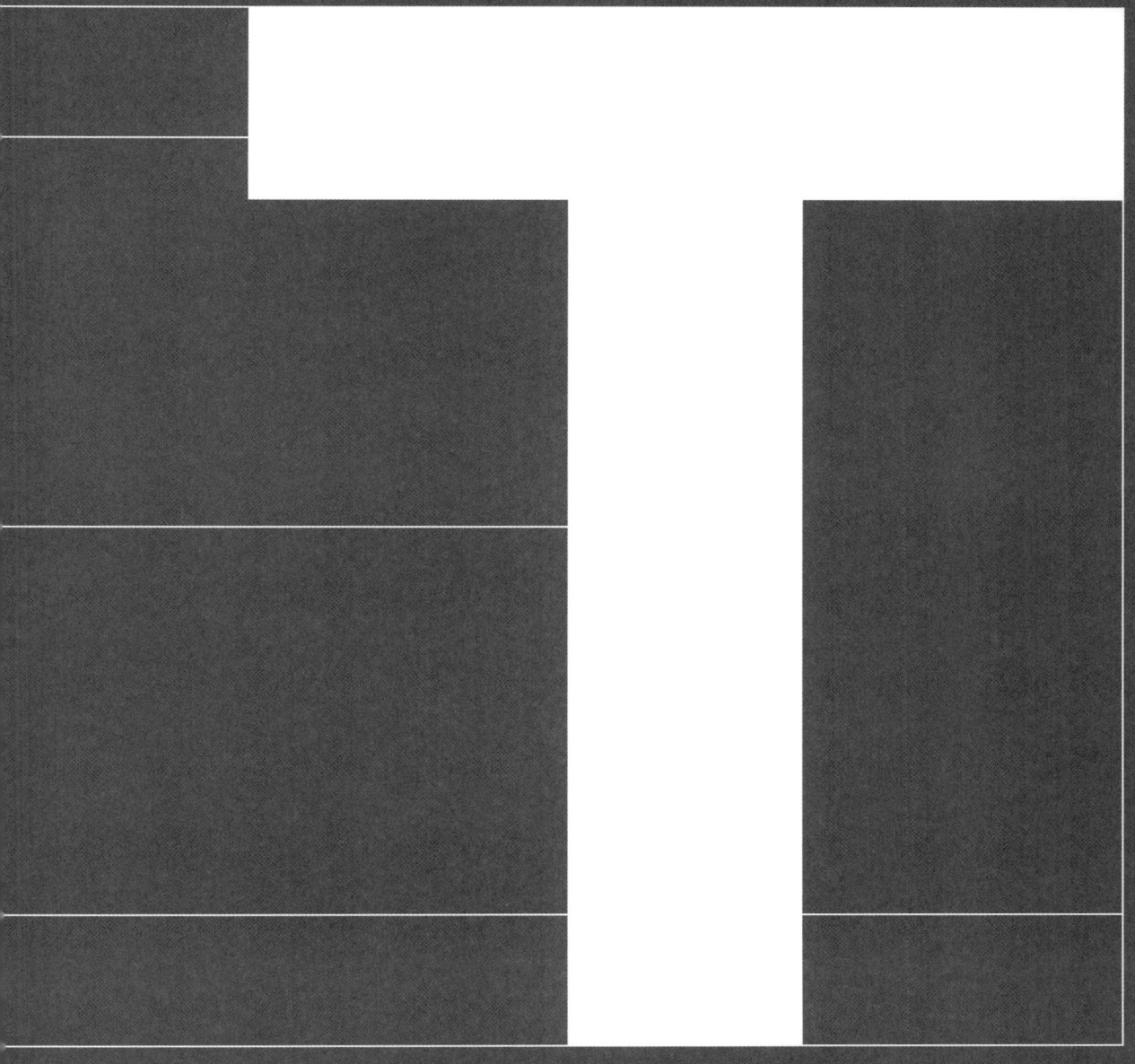

243

STAN   SMITH   80S   "MASTER   YODA"   2011

THE MOST

PETRA   COLLINS

PETRA   COLLINS

T

is for The Most Attention

"Stan Smith (the shoe) is easy—it doesn't command attention but it gets attention. I've always loved them for that quality, that ease. I dress for comfort, so I can glide through the world and through my sets like an athlete would. Stan Smiths allow me that."

Petra Collins
Artist and Curator

COME WHEN YOU

ATTENTION WILL

PETRA COLLINS   PETRA COLLINS

Petra Collins, 2018. *Opposite:* Stan Smith embodying the athleticism of the shoe, 1971.

LEAST EXPECT IT

THE CITY THAT

NEW YORK CITY NEW YORK CITY

T
is for The City

Just find them on the street. That was the assignment. Not only am I gonna find this one particular sneaker on the street, but also I'm gonna chase it and somehow make a nice photo of it without getting beaten up? Right. But man, all it took was setting foot in Herald Square, a.k.a. the Stan Smith capital of New York, and looking down. If Stan Smiths were slot machine cherries, you'd be a millionaire, day one. It's nuts. Every pattern and shade criss-crossing the intersection, at all hours. Turns out the only cause for self-pity is the alarm that's gonna go off in my head for the next 10 years every time I see a pair of Stan Smiths.

Daniel Arnold
Photographer

WALKS IN A

NEVER   SLEEPS

NEW   YORK   CITY   NEW   YORK   CITY

LOT   OF   STANS

THE

JEFFERSON HACK

EFFORTLESS ELEGANCE

TIMELESS

is for The Timeless Elegance

The Stan Smith is a modern design classic. No shoe has such countercultural DNA. No shoe has transcended fashion cycles, music genres, design trends as effortlessly as the Stan Smith. Its power is in its simplicity, its elegance, in its timeless, egalitarian silhouette. It says you have taste that you know design, that you understand cultural value, even if you don't know that it does.

Jefferson Hack
Co-Founder and Editorial Director, Dazed Media

OF COUNTERCULTURE

TWENTY - TWO

WORLD RECORD   WORLD RECORD

"This James Bond–inspired mural was in the adidas lounge at Roland Garros for the whole tournament, much to my wife's embarrassment." – S.S.

TO   THROW

MILLION REASONS

WORLD RECORD   WORLD RECORD

T
is for Twenty-Two Million

Two hundred guests were invited to a party in the adidas lounge at Roland Garros and were given a pair of my shoes to wear for the occasion. A representative from Guinness World Records then presented the adidas boss with a certificate stating that the Stan Smith shoe had sold more pairs than any other "named" shoe: twenty-two million. Robert Haillet, the former French No. 1, attended the occasion. He and Horst Dassler created the shoe and his name was the first name on it. Both our names were then on the shoe for about four years, and then his name gradually was dropped. – S.S

Official Guinness World Record certificate, 1989.

A PARTY

ADIDAS ORIGINALS

252

ADIDAS ORIGINALS

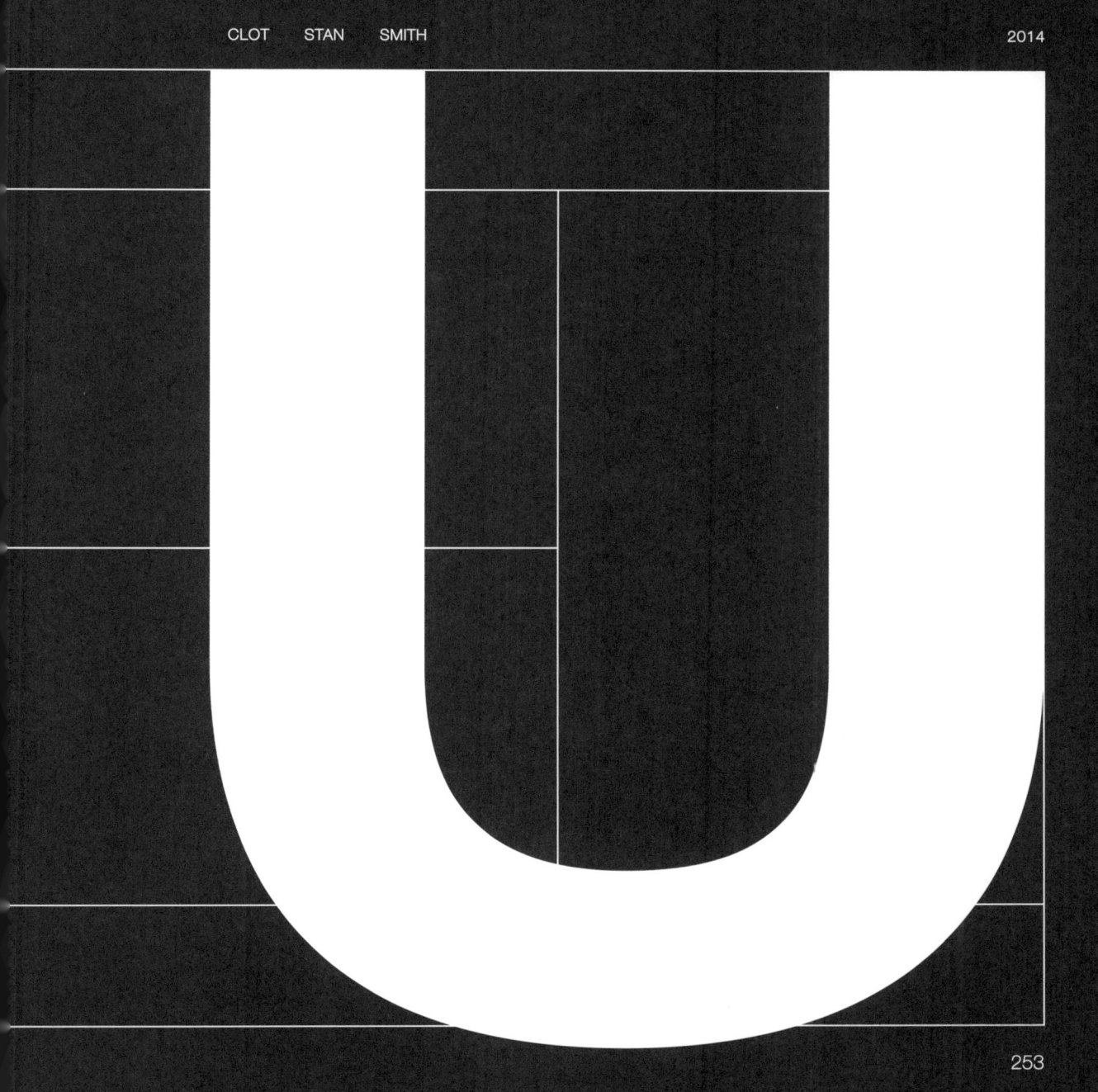

CLOT   STAN   SMITH   2014

U

253

CLOT   STAN   SMITH   2014

UNDER THE

WIMBLEDON 1966

U
is for Under The Lights

In 1966, I got a life lesson playing at Wimbledon. I was drawn against a young English player called Keith Wooldridge and we were given the privilege of playing on the Centre Court, where neither of us had played before. Walking out I wondered how I was going to handle it. But when I served, Keith's return sailed back over my head. He was so nervous he could barely walk. Suddenly, I realized he must be in worse shape than I was. The life lesson was clear: stop worrying about how nervous you feel and all your problems, and realize that others might have more issues than you, whether in life or in a tennis match. – S.S.

WIMBLEDON 1966

A STOMACH FULL

LIGHTS　　　WITH

WIMBLEDON　1966　　　　　　　　WIMBLEDON　1966

255

OF　　　BUTTERFLIES

UNITING   THREE

AN   ANSWER   IN   ITSELF   AN   ANSWER   IN   ITSELF

U

is for Uniting

I change colors for the seasons. Winter is black; spring is usually navy; summer is blue. Depending on my mood I change silhouettes and style a bit. When I do that I can be sure the Stan Smith will always fit the new style. So, to be honest, no deep meaning—just the versatility of it.
My father had a box of Stan Smiths; so do I and so does my wife. I am pretty certain that when the kids grow up, they will do the same.

Choosing a Stan Smith is like waking up and washing your face in the morning. No reason why it is like that, but in a certain way, you could say that is an answer in itself. Trying to create a design that is better than the Stan Smith is almost impossible, I think.

Yosuke Aizawa
Designer, White Mountaineering

WHAT'S   ON

GENERATIONS BY

AN ANSWER IN ITSELF AN ANSWER IN ITSELF

adidas Originals x White Mountaineering
Stan Smith, 2015

THEIR FEET

ADIDAS   ORIGINALS   X   JEREMY   SCOTT

258

ADIDAS   ORIGINALS   X   JEREMY   SCOTT

STAN   SMITH   "SUBWAY"   2015

STAN   SMITH   "SUBWAY"   2015

VICTORY CREATES

VIRGINIA WADE   VIRGINIA WADE

V

is for Victory

The final of the 1972 gentlemen's singles at Wimbledon will always be one of the most memorable to me! It was rain-delayed, postponed from the traditional Saturday until Sunday, and all of us Wimbledon players still in London were ready for a celebration. That day, we were lunch guests at the elegant London home of John Dewar, of Dewar's whisky and a big sponsor of tennis. Of course, we all wanted to watch the men's final, a spellbinding affair that went up and down for hours, and finally was won by the classy American Stan Smith! He looked the epitome of a tennis player: tall, sleek, athletic, and sportsmanlike. Right out of central casting!

It was the very early days of sponsorship, so who better for adidas to use as their brand carrier! The Stan Smith shoes were catapulted into the marketplace! Along with Rod Laver's line, a history of tennis shoes developed. Gradually, what we had always used as tennis shoes, the white canvas sneakers, were being replaced by state-of-the-art leather athletic shoes. Through all these decades, the iconic Stan Smith shoes have survived and had a total rebirth in street culture and celebrity culture, and today are a must-have for any trendy wardrobe. I was reading about a sneakerhead recently who has over four hundred pairs of collectable sneakers in her collection; I can only assume she has dozens of Stan Smiths. What a success story!

Virginia Wade
Tennis champion

CLASS MAKES

THE CHAMPION

VIRGINIA WADE

CHAMPION

VIRGINIA WADE

Opposite: The last time that Queen Elizabeth II visited Wimbledon in 1977, hometown favorite Virgina Wade took the crown—and plate.

261

THE

LEGEND

VERY

BOOST

V

is for Very Comfortable

How do you improve a classic like the Stan Smith? Easy, give it a BOOST sole. For decades sports shoe brands had searched for a sole material that was soft enough to provide a comfortable ride but also had the perfect amount of springiness to return energy to the foot. When adidas teamed up with chemical giants BASF, they found it in the form of a sole made of thousands of small pellets of a very clever material called Thermoplastic Polyurethane.

When it was first applied to adidas running shoes, the newly named BOOST proved such an unprecedented success that the brand could barely keep up with the demand. It wasn't long before Stan Smith fans began dreaming of a BOOST-equipped Stan Smith, wondering if adidas would ever bring the classic shoe and BOOST together.

In early 2017, adidas made Stan Smith fans dreams come true. Many hailed it as a sign of respect for its fans and a recognition by adidas of the Stan Smith's position as one of its crown jewels. The Stan Smith BOOST was the perfect melding of a classic design with the very latest technology. Just as it had been at the time of its creation, the Stan Smith was once again on the cutting edge of sports shoe technology.

Jason Coles

VERY   VERY

BOOST   BOOST

adidas Originals x Sneakersnstuff
Stan Smith BOOST "Shades Of
White V2", 2017

COMFORTABLE

VERSATILITY IS

SACHA JENKINS

V

is for Versatility

Hip-hop and a shoe? A shoe called Stan Smith? Unlikely as it would seem, is there a connection? Yes, and musician/TV producer/filmmaker Sacha Jenkins explains why.

"Hip-hop grew on the streets of Queens, New York, where I lived as a kid in the 1970s," says Jenkins. "It was played outside, drawing everyone in, reflecting the society we were living in. And it became language, a universal language because it became aligned with fashion. How you dressed revealed who you were. I could tell if someone came from Brooklyn by the way they dressed."

SACHA JENKINS

One of the original hip-hop groups, Run-DMC was emerging in Queens at the same time and they began to set the tone for how young people dressed. "And footwear was at the foundation of that," notes Jenkins. "Shoes became a sub-culture and set the tone. DMC wanted to draw people in and make everyone feel comfortable—like, 'I can know these guys; I can talk to these guys,' so what they wore was clean, simple, and solid, something that could be worn with anything."

By the mid 1990s, fashion styles began edging shoe popularity away from the Superstar basketball shoe, and adidas was at the forefront of that. Branding became important and collaboration between music—hip-hop, rap—and sneakers soon became big business.

"It was then that the Stan Smith adidas became hip-hop's favorite footwear," Jenkins explained. "In hip-hop, fashion is language and because the Stan Smith was so clean and versatile it spoke many languages. It still does and will continue to do so."

Opposite: The Beastie Boys, New York City, 1986.

THAT KEEPS YOU

THE LANGUAGE

SACHA JENKINS

HOT FOR DECADES

ADIDAS PHARRELL WILLIAMS

266

ADIDAS

HU HOLI STAN SMITH MC								2018

HU HOLI STAN SMITH MC								2018

WHEN STAN KEPT

TONGUE WAG   TONGUE WAG

W
is for When Stan Kept it Calm

Part of the beauty of the Stan Smiths' design is that it was almost perfect from day one, meaning t has had very few changes to it over time. But among the few that have been made was one of the smallest, yet most important. It was also requested by Stan himself. Early models of the shoe could suffer from "tongue wag" during play, meaning the tongue of the shoe would move slightly to one side. Stan requested that two perforations be added that allowed the laces to be looped through the tongue, stopping it from moving and making the shoe even more comfortable to wear during matches.

Jason Coles

Originally, the tongue would move to one side of the other. The loop addition kept it in place. *Opposite:* Showing off the shoe to photographers, 2014.

STOPPED TONGUES

IT   CALM   AND

TONGUE   WAG   TONGUE   WAG

269

FROM   WAGGING

W

is for Wimbledon's Grass

I thought I should have been given a spot in the main draw at Wimbledon in 1964. There were no computer rankings in those days and tournament committees were only guided by results sent in from a player's federation. I had won the USA Junior title at Kalamazoo and felt that should have been good enough to get me straight in. But, no, it was off to Roehampton for the qualifying, where I led a British guy called Geoff Bluett by two sets to love and lost. You could say I blew it! Good joke, but I wasn't too happy at having missed out on my first attempt to play at Wimbledon. Then, a strange thing happened: a veteran American player called Herbie Flam had been practicing with me in LA in an attempt to get his game back together after a long layoff. Because of an excellent past record, Wimbledon put him in the draw. But at the last moment he got too nervous and pulled out. I was the next man in! So, I got to play a guy from Holland and won. The great Mexican, Rafael Osuna, who had won the U.S. title the year before, was my next opponent and, unsurprisingly, I lost. But it was a start!

Replica of the Wimbledon men's trophy. *Opposite:* Margie and me celebrating my Wimbledon victory, 1972.

GRASS IS

WIMBLEDON ENTRY   WIMBLEDON ENTRY

LITTLE   GREENER

WIMBLEDON ENTRY

WIMBLEDON ENTRY

This is the "President's Cup," it reads: "All England Lawn Tennis Club, Wimbledon, The President's Cup 1972, All Comers Singles, Championship of the World, Stan Smith."
– S.S.

One of the three Wimbledon trophies you get when you win the singles title. This one memorializes William Renshaw, an Englishman, who won seven Wimbledon championships.

WIMBLEDON ENTRY

"I jumped over the net after winning Wimbledon in 1972." – S.S.

WHEN YOU GET

MAC CATO

W

is for When You Get a Present

My first view of Stan's size 13 shoes was next to the single bed in my son's room. In the late '60s and early '70s young tennis players were often hosted by families when they followed the tour to London. Stan endured this single bed every time he came through London, through a loss to John Newcombe in the 1972 Wimbledon finals, and a triumphal victory over Nastase in the 1973 finals. I first met Margie Smith in 1972, when she was playing in a Wimbledon qualifying tournament; Stan and I hid and watched the match from beyond the fencing, much to her dismay. She extracted her revenge on me by consistently beating

me whenever and wherever we had a chance to play. But we shared more than a few nervous moments over the years as spectators at Stan's matches. Of course, Stan's warrior's shoes subsequently took him all over the world, sometimes winning, sometimes losing, but always conducting himself like the gentleman he is. I was always delighted when Stan and I had the chance to get together—I still am, although the chance to do so occurs less often since I moved back from London. However, our friendship remains as durable as his shoes! I spent a career working in branding for world-class products and I know real quality when it's there. Stan Smith has always been a worthy champion.

Mac Cato
Family Friend

IF YOU WIN

A PRESENT ONLY

MAC CATO MAC CATO

"A drawing that Mac Cato left in my hotel, with instructions to the concierge to deliver only if I won the US Open Finals." – S.S.

275

THE OPEN

WAREHOUSES CAN

CRAIG KALLMAN

276

YOU OWN

BE CLOSETS IF

CRAIG KALLMAN   CRAIG KALLMAN

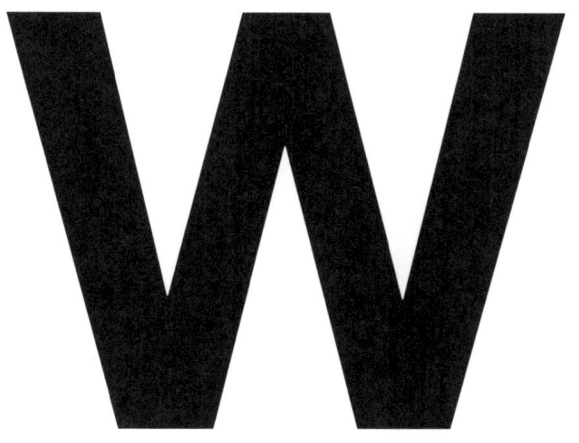

W
is for Warehouses

Craig Kallman, chairman of Atlantic Records, has been wearing the Stan Smith shoe since childhood.

"I remember having to find the smallest adult size," Kallman recalls. "I liked the Stan Smith because it was elegant and simple and really comfortable to wear."

So much so that Craig never looked for anything else. "I'm a creature of habit and, honestly, I have never worn another kind of sneaker. I became known in the music industry as the guy wearing Stan Smiths in all the photos. And it wasn't cool.

When hip-hop exploded and fashion lifestyle became all about sneakers, I used to take a lot of abuse. There were some crazy designs out there and I was still in my Stan Smiths."

For a while it looked as if Stan Smiths would disappear off the market altogether anc Craig panicked. "I did!" he says earnestly. "I thought life is ending as I know it. I won't be able to find any more Stan Smiths! So, I thought the only solution was to buy up every pair of size 10 Stan Smiths I could lay my hands on."

Kallman was talking literally and globally and with the resources at his disposal to back up his manic scheme. "I had my executives in Warner territories around the world—in the U.S., Europe, and Japan—scour local markets for size 10 Stan Smiths. And they found plenty. I had warehouses ready because I am a big vinyl collector and there was space for the Stan Smith sneakers as they started arriving. At a guess, I reckon I must have had about six or seven hundred with all colors on the back splash—green, blue, red. Still do. But then, of course, everything changed."

Suddenly, the abuse stopped and the chairman was the coolest guy around. His favorite shoe had become everyone's favorite shoe, so he no longer needed to explain what Kallman calls "this gorgeous sneaker."

Opposite: A small sampling of Craig Kallman's several hundred pairs of Stan Smith's that are stashed across multiple warehouses.

700 STANS

ADIDAS CONSORTIUM X NEIGHBORHOOD

STAN　　SMITH　　　　　　　　　　　　　　　　　　　　　　　　2014

STAN　　SMITH　　　　　　　　　　　　　　　　　　　　　　　　2014

X FACTORS ARE

DAVIS CUP DAVIS CUP

Clockwise from top left: Freddie McNair, trainer Bill Norris, Brian Gottfried, Bob Lutz, Dr. Omar Fareed, me, Roscoe Tanner, Arthur Ashe, and Captain Tony Trabert, Davis Cup team, 1974.

A TEAM

X

is for X Factors

My Davis Cup ambitions began to be realized in 1968, when I played doubles with Bob Lutz on the team that beat Australia in the final in Adelaide. From then on, I was a member of seven winning campaigns over twelve years. We also reached the final in 1973, by which time open tennis had arrived. That meant the Australians could pick their best players. Embarrassed by riches, their captain Neale Fraser was able to leave Ken Rosewall on the bench at an indoor final in Cleveland. We lost 5–0 even though the first two singles matches went to five sets. The opposition consisted of Rod Laver and John Newcombe! – S.S.

"Replica of the Davis Cup trophy that I received when I was a Davis Cup ambassador in 2000." – S.S.

X IS

UNDEFEATED

is for X is the Spot

I grew up in Philadelphia at the time when adidas was the superstar of the sportswear industry. I first noticed the Stan Smith shoe in my early twenties. It hit the market as the classic, clean shoe, all white with the green hit on the back. It was perfect for the preppy '80s.

It has survived and become a fashion item because now fashion rules over function. But the Stan Smith scores with both. Here in LA, you can wear it for every occasion. You can go to a business meeting in your Stan Smiths or you can go skating in them because they are so well constructed.

UNDEFEATED

I think one of the biggest reasons for its continued success is that the Stan Smith, in a highly competitive market, is unthreatened by anything. In a fashion and, of course, in a technical sense, it never makes you feel uncomfortable. There is nothing else like it. And it is timeless.

James Bond
Co-Founder, UNDEFEATED

THAT NEVER MAKES

THE SPOT

UNDEFEATED UNDEFEATED

adidas Originals x Bedwin x Beauty & Youth and United Arrows x Undefeated, 2010.

YOU UNCOMFORTABLE

ADIDAS CONSORTIUM X Y'S BY YOHJI YAMAMOTO

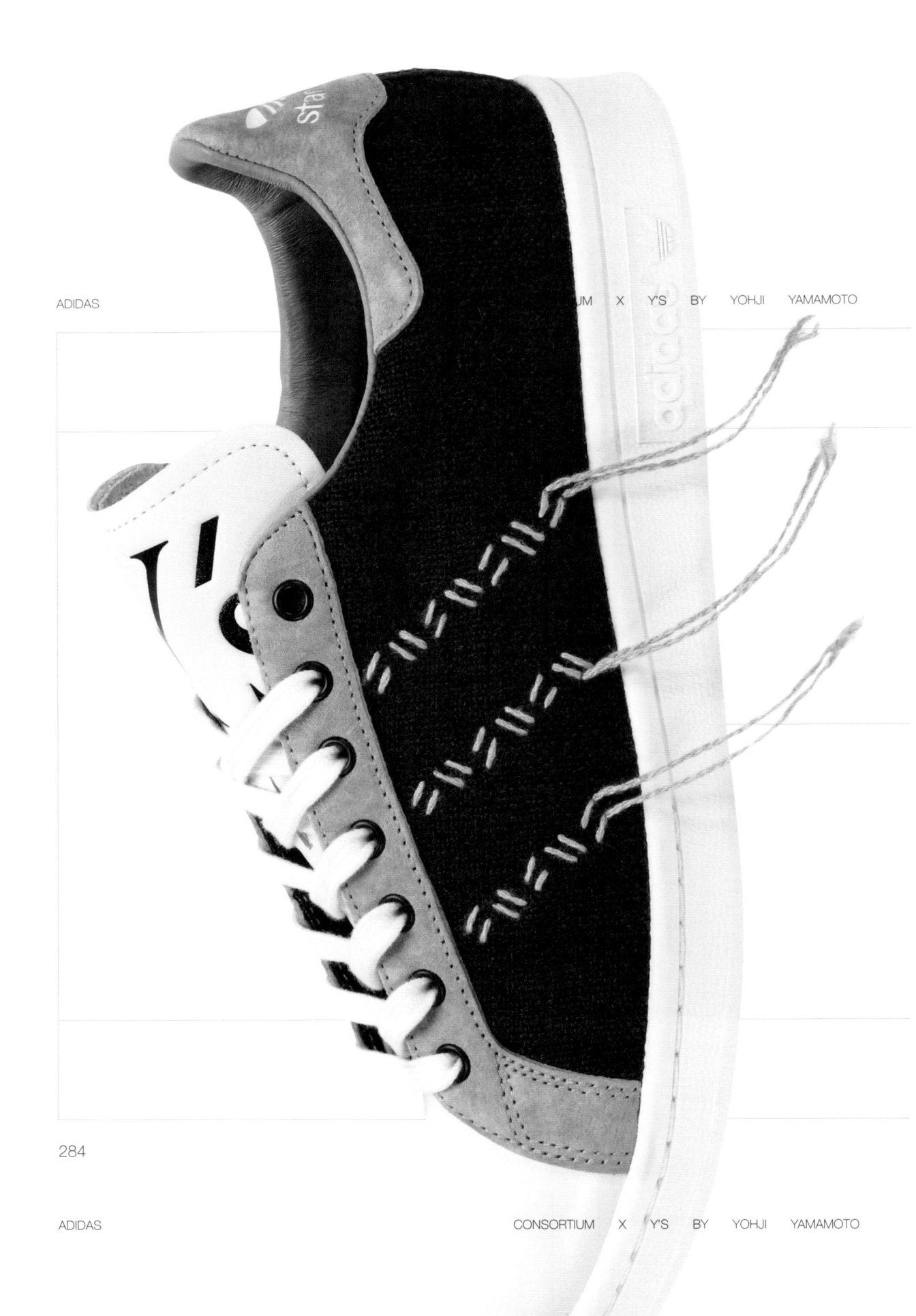

284

ADIDAS CONSORTIUM X Y'S BY YOHJI YAMAMOTO

STAN   SMITH   2014

285

STAN   SMITH   2014

PRIMEKNIT

Y

is for Yarn

Inspired by adidas athletes who wanted a shoe made from a material that was durable but as light as a feather, Primeknit was created by digitally knitting fused yarn to create an entire upper in just one piece. Ultra-lightweight and flexible, a Primeknit upper seamlessly wraps around the foot like a sock, providing a level of comfort that means it goes almost unnoticed by the wearer. However, when adidas first brought the Stan Smith and Primeknit together, it's true to say that some fans were initially skeptical. That is, until they tried it on. Even the most stalwart fans of the original were impressed by how adidas's designers had managed to craft the classic Stan Smith shape in Primeknit and marry it to the original shoe's much-loved sole unit, making it one of the most comfortable Stan Smiths ever made.

Jason Coles

THE · FUTURE

PRIMEKNIT · PRIMEKNIT

adidas Originals Stan Smith Prime Knit, Mid White/White, Wonder Pink, White/Green, 2017.

287

THE · PAST

YOU NEVER KNOW

IN PERPETUITY IN PERPETUITY

Y

is for You Never Know

Serving as Davis Cup captain in 1968 and 1969 were two of my happiest years in tennis. Stan had a big hand in that happiness, as he had just graduated with Bob Lutz from the University of Southern California as a twenty-one year old and he formed the backbone of the winning Davis Cup teams in 1968 and 1969. He and Bob never lost a Cup doubles match in those two years. Stan and Bob went on to win twelve Grand Slam doubles titles over the next decade.

However, Stan emerged in the early 1970s as a towering figure in winning singles titles over the world, such as the U.S. Open in 1971 and Wimbledon in 1972, beating Nastase in a five-set classic battle. That summer, Stan went on a tear winning eight pro titles, including Wimbledon and Davis Cup finals on clay in Romania.

My wife, Carole, when asked by Life magazine in 1972 who would she pick to win "if her life depended on it," she, without any hesitation, replied, "Stan Smith." That was Stan's trademark—a cool, calm assassin on grass and hard courts. Stan dominated all tennis in 1972 and finished ranked No. 1 in the world.

Three weeks after winning Wimbledon in 1972, Horst Dassler phoned me and said that he wanted Stan to endorse his newly developed all-leather shoe. I responded in a smart aleck way: "But, Horst, you can't afford him." How wrong I was, and that began a forty-seven-year endorsement with adidas—the longest and most lucrative relationship in sports shoe history. Recently Stan agreed to sign a new, lasting contract in perpetuity for his worldwide popular white leather Stan Smith shoe—hopefully for another forty-seven years or longer.

I have always admired Stan's character, strong beliefs, and values. We first bonded on our undefeated Davis Cup team, and based on our mutual trust and friendship we have worked together as lawyer/client on a simple handshake, representing Stan in all his business affairs. It's been a long, successful ride with Stan, Margie, and his four children and it's not over yet—indeed there are many challenges (and shoes) ahead.

Donald Dell
Stan's Agent and Dear Friend

HERR HORST

WHAT HAPPENS WHEN

IN PERPETUITY   IN PERPETUITY

Stan and Donald Dell, 1974. *Opposite:* Gold bracelet that Donald gave to Stan in the mid-80s, commemorating his four U.S. Open Doubles Championships.

289

DASSLER CALLS

YEAR AFTER

STAN FANS · STAN FANS

Y

is for Year After Year

"Stan Smith is an icon not only in the sports world, but also in the world of shoes. His staple sneakers he created with adidas forty years ago have secured his spot as footwear royalty and a staple in my everyday style. I am and will forever be a Stan Smith sneaker mega fan."

Hailey Baldwin
Model, New York, USA

"A few months ago, while walking around the shopping mall, we went to the adidas store. Jake went for a walk around the store and I met him at the stand with children's Stan Smiths. Jake showed me a pair of shoes and immediately tried it on. I didn't think anything of it and left the store. A week later we were in the same store and Jake purposefully went to the same pair of shoes again. Everything was decided. Now he won't wear anything else to walk in."

Weng San Lo
Jake Fu's Parent, Hong Kong

adidas Originals Stan Smith Baby, 2018.

WINS FAN

YEAR STAN AFTER FAN

STAN FANS

"When I think of the Stan Smith, I instantly think back to when my older cousins used to cruise around in a pair of these when I was growing up in the '90s. I just remembered being really young and wondering what those shoes were. That pair of white shoes with that dude's face printed on the tongue is what I remembered as a cartoon-loving child. So, not even knowing who the guy on the tongue was . . . I just wanted the shoe with "that cartoon guy" on the tongue . . . those white shoes that my cousin Charles and Steve wore around everywhere supporting this mysterious cartoon character. I was hoping to one day see a cartoon featuring this shoe tongue character and I never saw one. Instead, ten years later, I found out that "the cartoon dude" was the legendary tennis player, Stan Smith. It took me about ten years to realize that Stan Smith was a real person who played tennis in these shoes. Congrats Stan! The real one!"

Glenjamin
Photographer and Videographer,
Los Angeles, USA

STAN FANS

"I usually wear my pairs of Stans with cropped slacks from Kolor that have a prominent center crease and short sport socks that shows off the ankle. Basically, it's best to not go casual when styling the shoe, for me to feel most comfortable."

Junichi Abe
Kolor Designer, Tokyo, Japan

Top: adidas Originals Stan Smith
Reflective Heel, Maroon, 2016.

Bottom: adidas Originals Stan Smith
Silver Metallic, 2014.

ADIDAS

STAN SMITH

292

ADIDAS STAN SMITH

CONSORTIUM X JUICE 2016

CONSORTIUM X JUICE 2016

ZEN AND

ALLEN FOX

Z
is for Zen

Stan Smith did have a serene attitude on the court and he was quite dominating with it. I played him many times and that serene attitude of his was intimidating— even a little annoying, because it made you feel weak and ineffectual. The other players felt just like I did about Stan. He was (and is) religious and this somehow interacted with his confidence on court. But none of us could come up with anything he actually did that wrong. He was honest and a great competitor and no fun at all to play.

Allen Fox
Tennis champion

ALLEN FOX

Big Stan Smith (right) also took the singles title, beating Allen Fox in the final. Smith defeated Brian Cheney, Lutz and Tomaz Koch, while Fox downed Avoyer, Arilla and Riessen.

Allen Fox and me. *Opposite:* A Fischer racket promotion on a lake in Austria, 1982.

OF DRIVING YOUR

THE ART

ALLEN FOX ALLEN FOX

OPPONENTS CRAZY

ZILLIONS IS

30   POUNDS   30   POUNDS

Z

is for Zillions

I was working with adidas in 1985, the year that we reached the seven-million mark in sales for the Stan Smith shoe.

In order to have something special to present to him on court, I came up with an idea to create a trophy-like award to commemorate this special milestone. Let's bronze a pair of Stan's shoes from his closet! So, working with Stan's wife, Margie, I asked her to send me a pair of his worn size 13s. What I didn't think of was how heavy a pair of bronzed size 13 shoes would be when we placed the shoes on top of the wooden base. The commemorative award weighed at least

With J. Wayne Richmond and my sons, Ramsey and Trevor, La Quinta, CA, 1985. *Opposite:* Bronzed shoes celebrating the sale of seven million pairs of Stans.

MATTER

ONLY A

30 POUNDS 30 POUNDS

thirty pounds, which was alright to carry with two hands but not with just one. When I walked on court with the tournament director Charlie Pasarell, I was handed the microphone to make the presentation by TV announcer and former player Barry McKay. I quickly realized that holding the trophy in one hand and the mic in the other was a problem. So, to the amusement of Barry, Charlie, and Stan, I struggled to honor Stan on national TV as I held up the heavy pair of bronzed size 13 shoes with one wobbly hand while grasping the microphone in the other.

It was a special day for me to be a participating in recognizing this special milestone in Stan's career— We now know that seven million pairs was just the start of what would become one of the most desired shoes by consumers for another thirty-three years—the Stan Smith shoe.

While the sales milestones are quite phenomenal, what stands out most for me is that Stan Smith, who has become a good friend, is the same great guy now as he was when he was No. 1 in the world. A humble and caring champion, on and off the court.

J. Wayne Richmond
Managing Director, Major Events USTA

OF TIME

STAN AND MARGIE

STAN SMITH: 15 STORIES

AT JUERGEN'S STUDIO

Portraits by Juergen Teller

1968:

College Love

Margie reminds me that she was a thirteen-year-old ball girl for a tournament match I played in her hometown. I really didn't notice her until we met in La Jolla, California, five years after. Then later I became the top-ranked player at the University of Southern California and she was No. 1 on the women's Princeton tennis team. I am wearing my USC letterman's jacket and she is wearing her Princeton letter sweater awarded only to captains of an undefeated team.

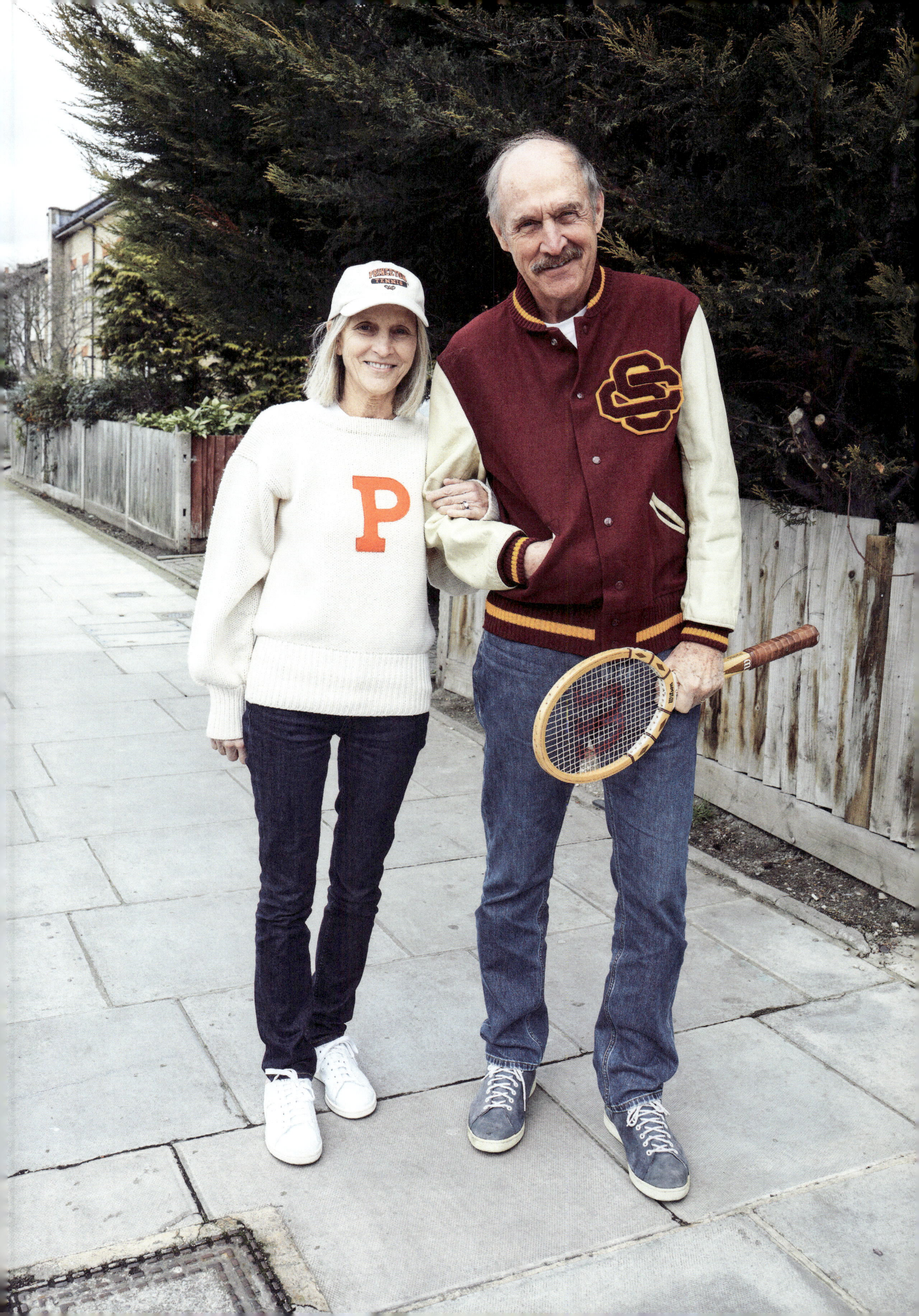

1970:

Drafted!

I'm wearing my original-issue jacket from when I was drafted into the Army in 1970. Back then the draft numbers were announced in the newspaper, and it was there that I saw my number was twenty-three. And therefore was immediately drafted, but was very lucky in that I still got to play tennis. While in the Army I won the U.S. Open and Wimbledon and traveled to Army bases and additional tournaments around the world. After two years, I processed out . . . but not without a scare after my dental records weren't found in the Active files but in the "DMF"—the Dead Man's File.

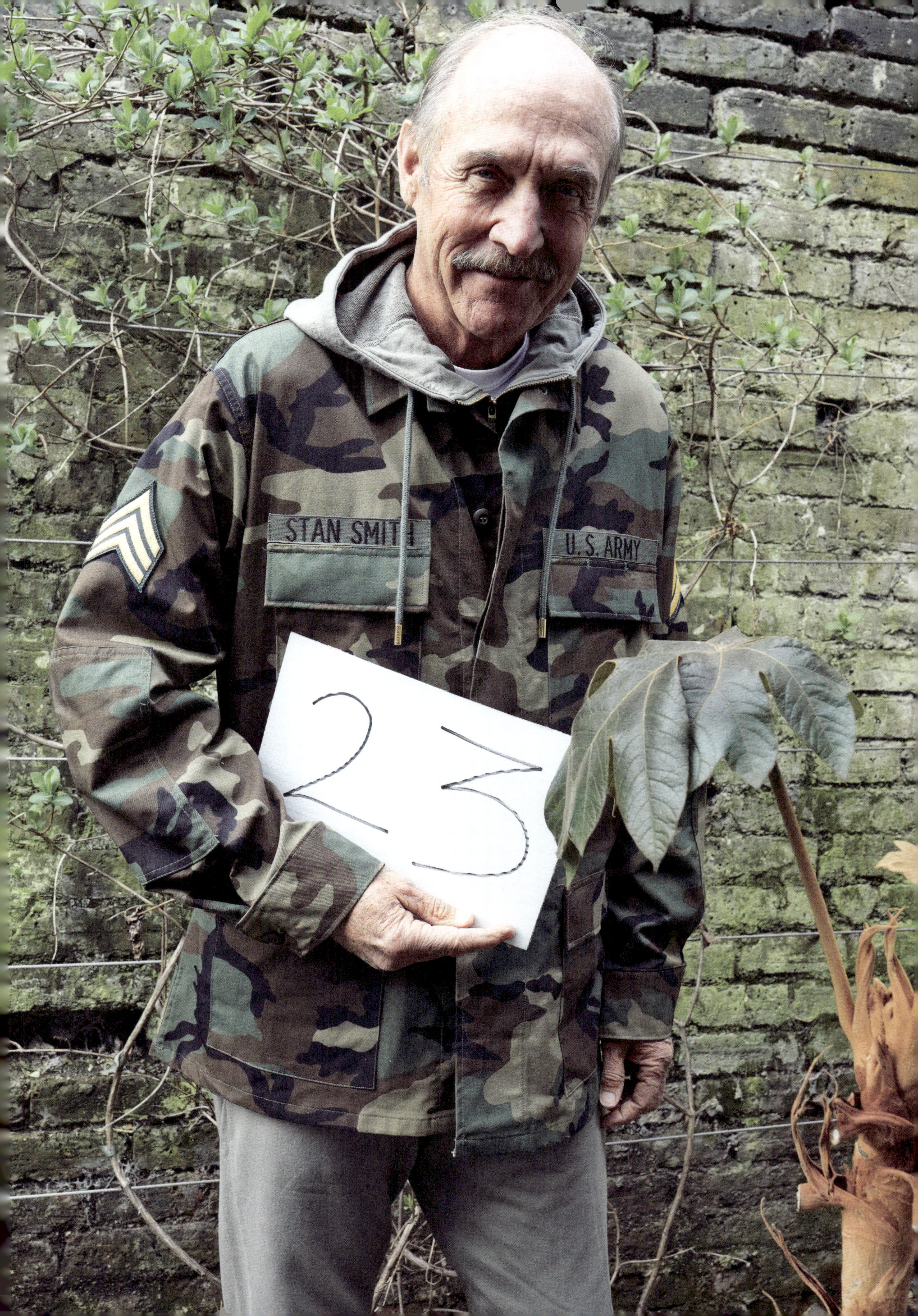
STAN SMITH
U.S. ARMY
23

1971:

Stans Before Stan

The Stan Smith shoe originally had another player's name on it—French tennis star Robert Haillet. In 1971, adidas wanted more exposure in the U.S. market and I was the logical choice since I was No. 1 in the U.S. and in the world at the time. I'm wearing a limited-edition adidas track suit matching the colors of the iconic shoe and holding an original deadstock pair of the shoe when it was known as the Robert Haillet. The towering stack of Originals shoe boxes represent the astronomical popularity and sales that the shoes reached once they became "Stans."

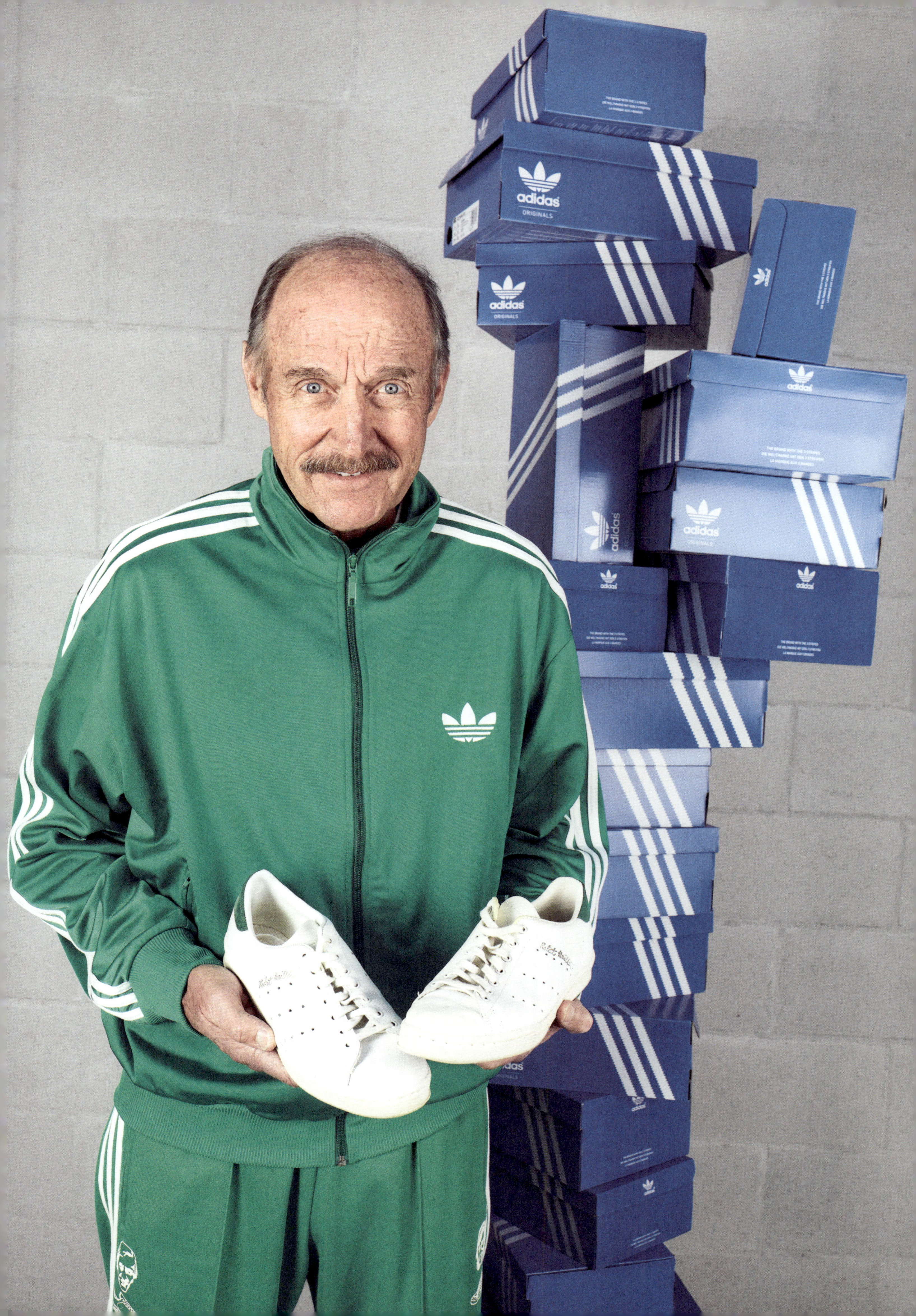
adidas
ORIGINALS

1972:

A Special Frenemy

Some of my most memorable battles on the tennis courts were against Ilie Nastase. Our personalities are completely opposite, as I am a cool, calm Californian while he is a fiery and emotional Romanian. He called me "Godzilla" and everyone playfully called him "Nasty." We faced each other many times in the 1970s, with the most epic instance being the notorious 1972 Davis Cup final in Nastase's native Bucharest and that year's Wimbledon Championship match. The limited-edition tracksuit commemorates our battles for the No. 1 ranking in the world. Over my shoulder is my signature Wilson racket, which I used in the 1970s.

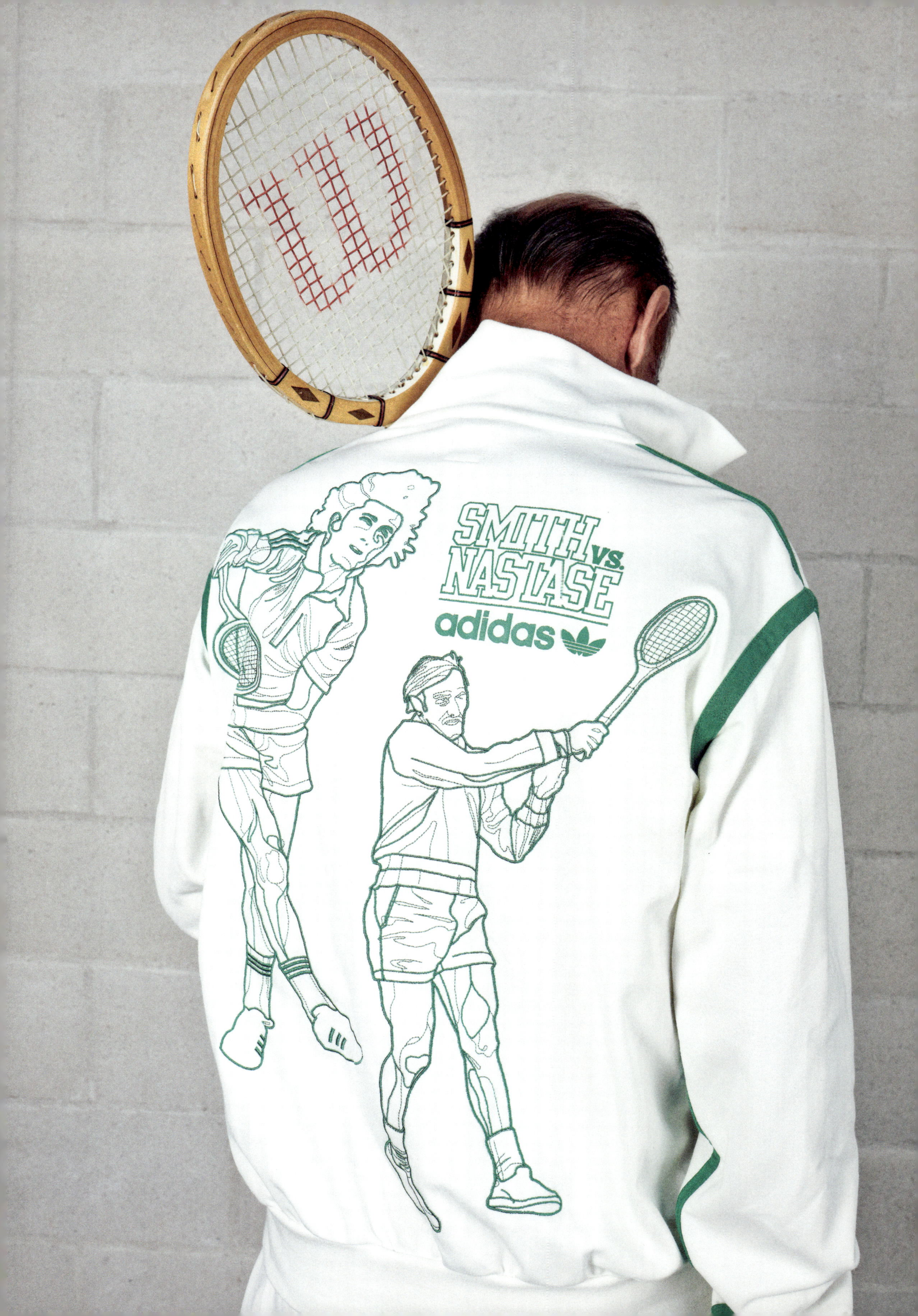
SMITH vs. NASTASE
adidas

1973:

Invisible Moustache

After college I always sported a moustache except for a brief period. It just happened that during that time I was photographed by adidas and this clean-shaven head shot was the one that they used for the shoe's tongue. I wonder sometimes if I should shave my moustache to look more like the shoe.

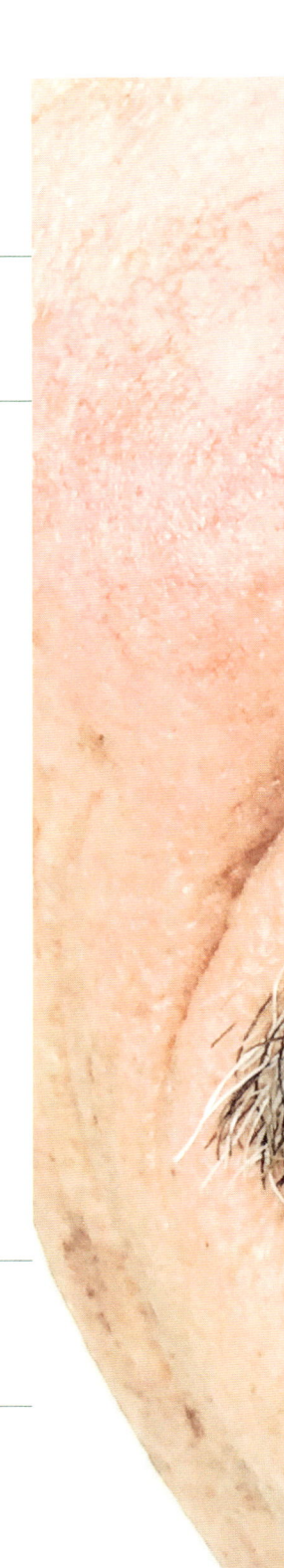

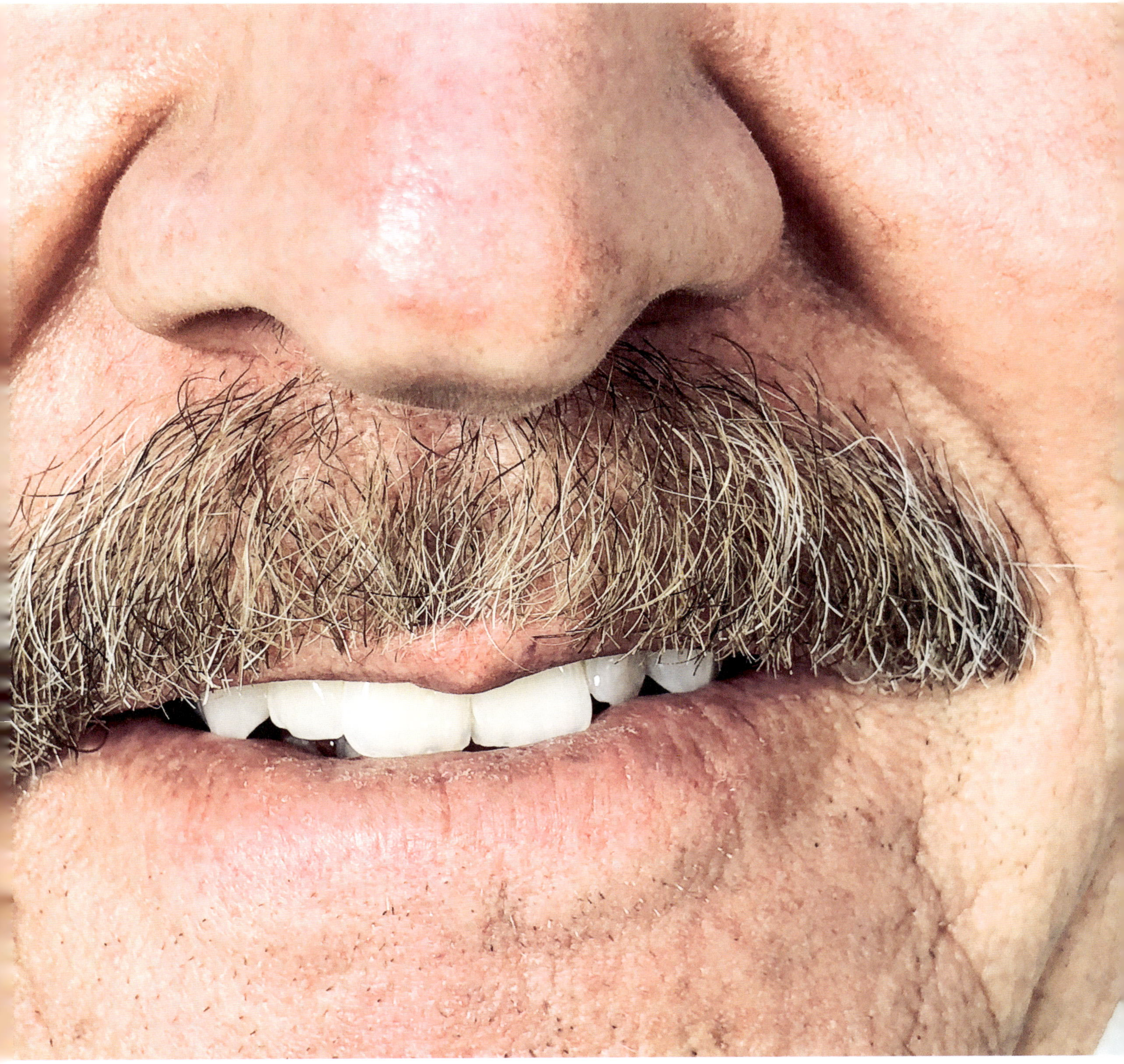

1976:

The Grandchildren Prophecy

Before we had kids, Margie and I were on the Paris Metro in 1976 when we saw a mother with a two- or three-year-old wearing the Stan Smith shoe. Margie, not knowing how long there would be a shoe with my name on it, remarked, "Wouldn't it be neat if one day our kids wore Stan Smith shoes?" Not only have all four of our kids grown up wearing the shoe, all thirteen grandchildren are wearing them, too. The shoe that I am holding is one that we bought for our first child.

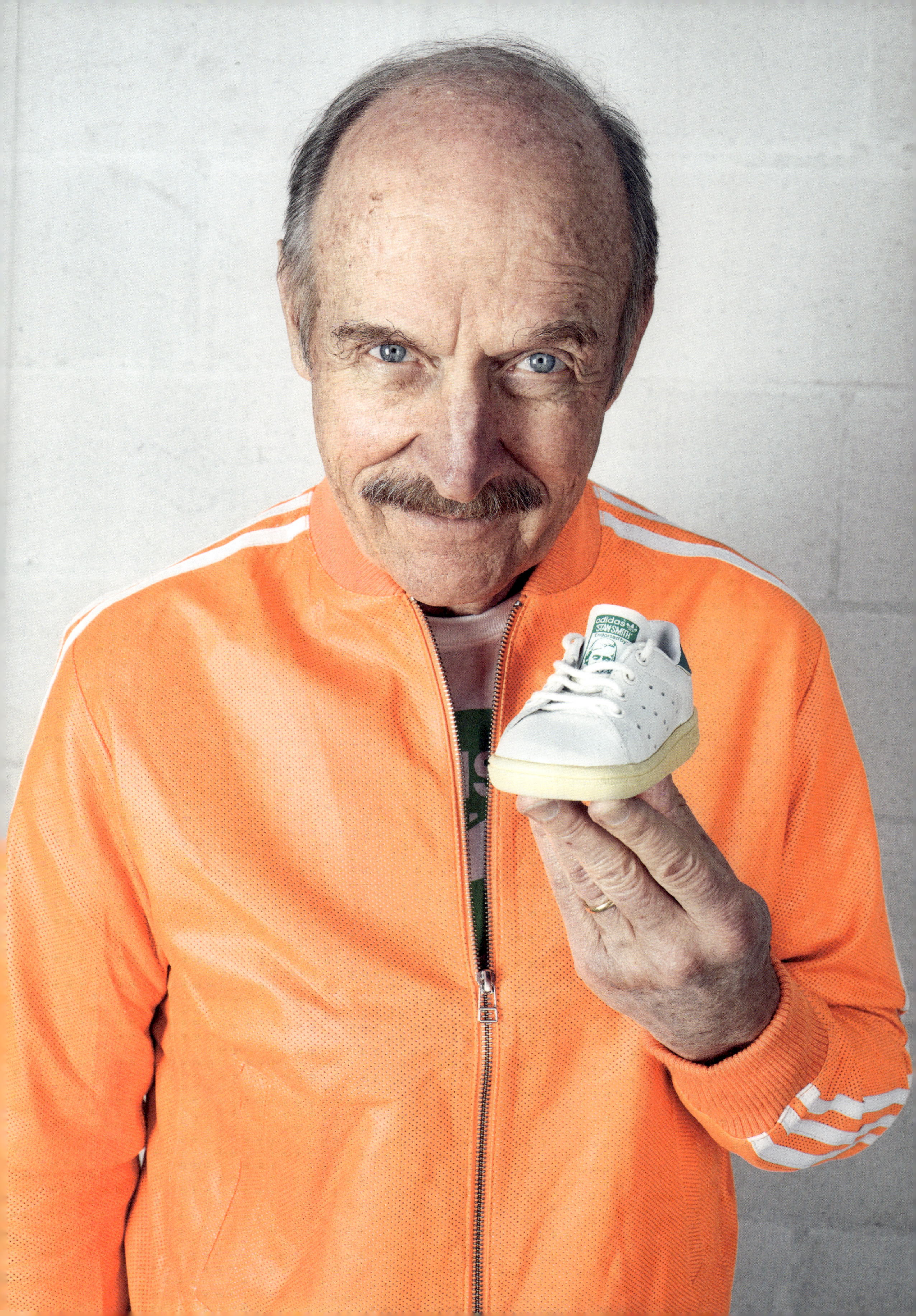

1977:

Wimbledon Plate

Winning Wimbledon was one of my four goals when I was sixteen years old. In this photo I am stretched out on real turf wearing a traditional tennis outfit from the era and holding a commemorative Centenary plate gifted to Wimbledon winners in 1977. The cup next to me is a replica of one of the most recognizable trophies in the world—the Wimbledon trophy. It is one of my prized possessions. Scattered in the grass are five coins, which were given to the finalists in doubles and a bronze coin, which I got for losing in the semifinal of singles in 1974. When I lost in the 1971 singles final I was so disappointed that I threw the coin on the locker room floor— it was returned years later.

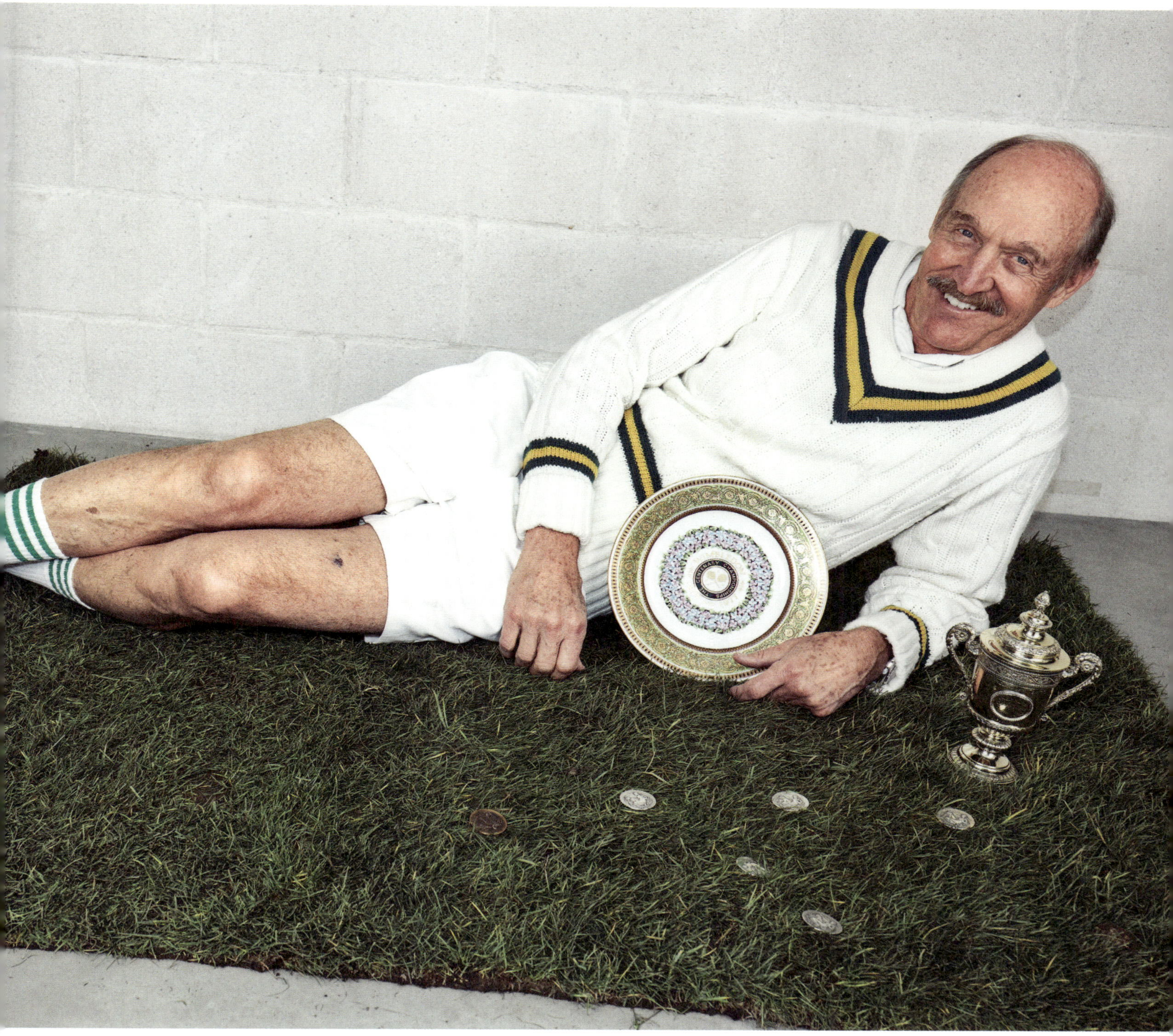

1985:

She Calls The Shots

Margie traveled with me during my career and got nervous watching me play. It is a helpless feeling just sitting in the stands cheering hard, but having no control over the outcome. She often wished she could call the lines instead of the umpire. Here she is finally sitting in the umpire's chair wearing her Stans and tennis outfit, but unfortunately I am not playing Wimbledon anymore.

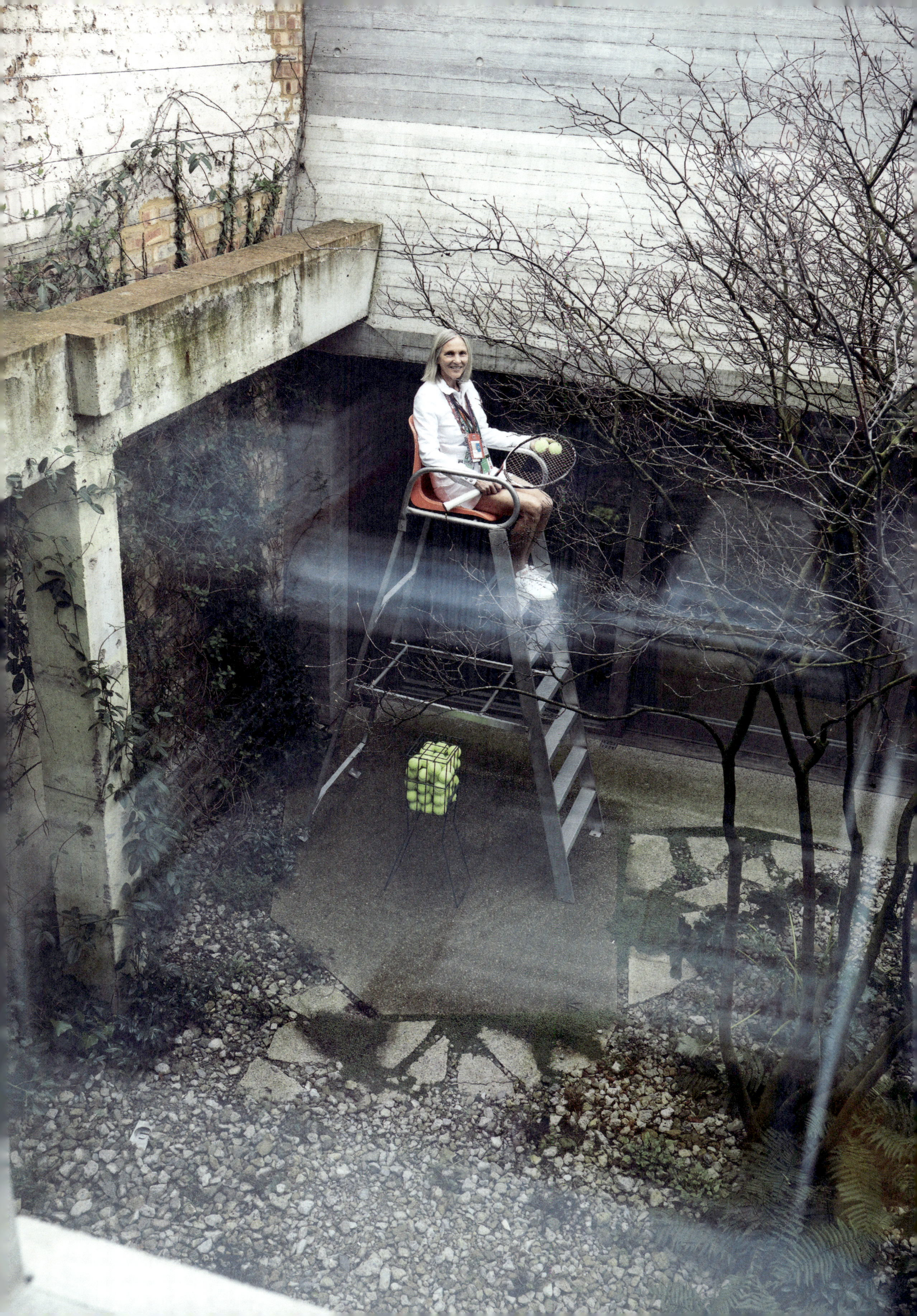

2002:

Coach Smith

Here I am in a typical pose as I give instruction to students at my tennis academy, which I started in 2002. It is located near my home at Sea Pines Resort on Hilton Head Island. It has been a real joy to work with young kids who love the game and desperately want to get better. It is important for them to realize that development is a slow and steady process and they can't learn the game overnight. The players hit many baskets of balls and work hard, but we have fun along the way.

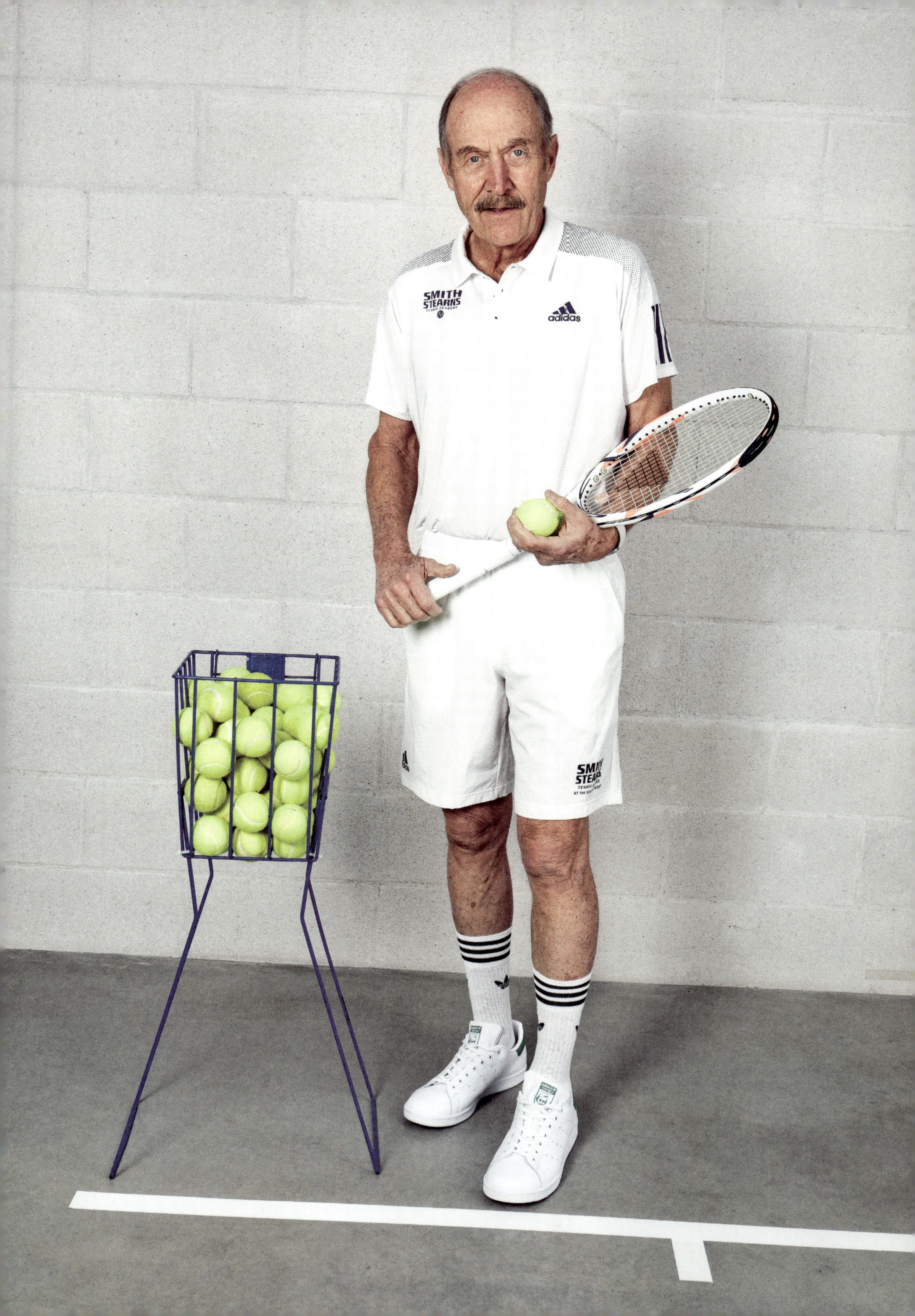
SMITH
STEARNS
adidas

2005:

Big in the Hood

In 2005, I was in New York City and going to a Prince party at a hotel before the start of the U.S. Open. When I arrived at the venue the parking attendant asked my name. After hearing my name and connecting it with the shoe, he said he would keep the car in front of the hotel so I could leave quickly. When I came out the valet was holding a pair of my shoes, which he happened to have in his office and asked me to sign them. He said that he was a big fan of the shoe and that they were "big in the hood."

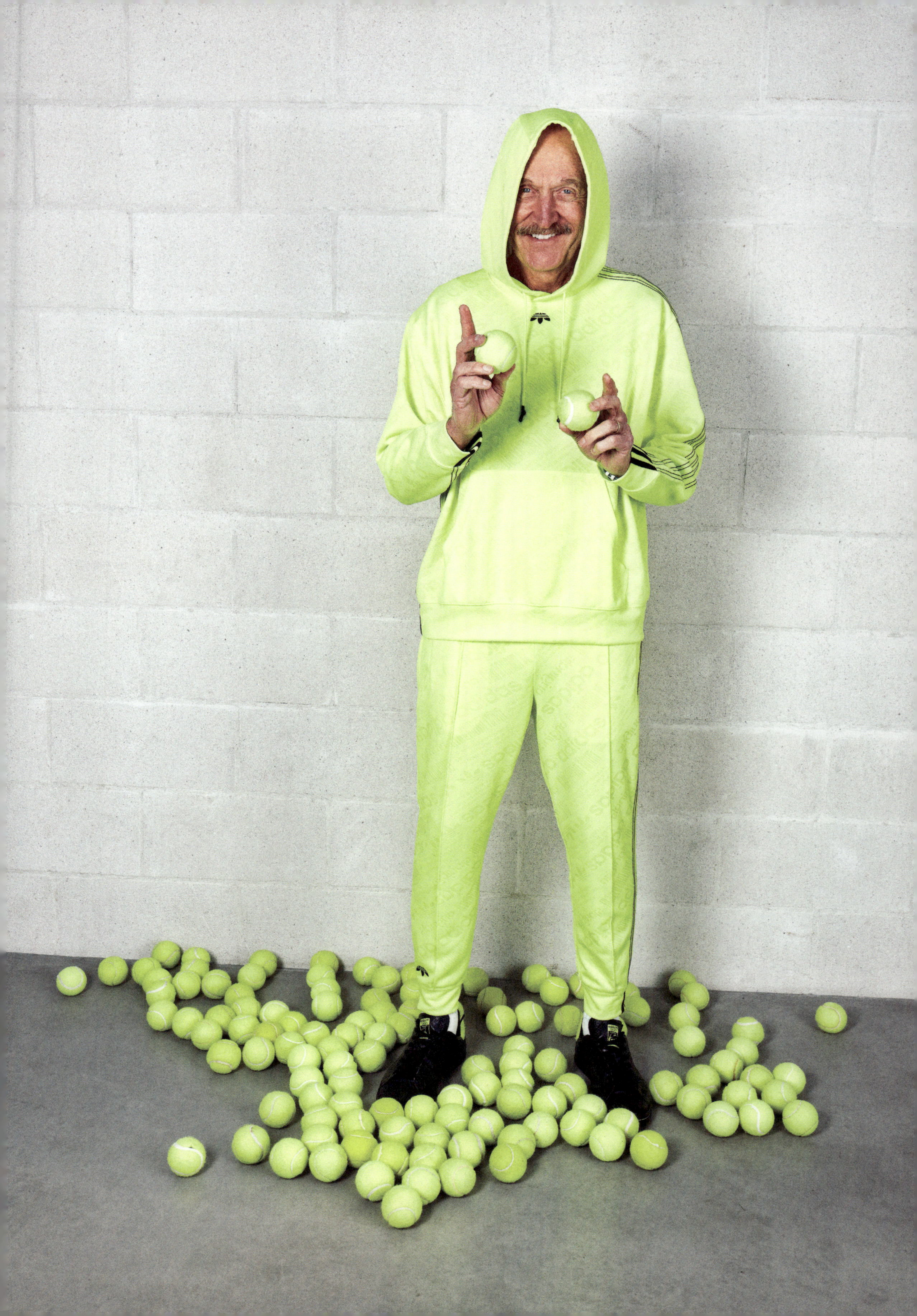

2010:

Hands Full of Stories

As I traveled around the world and was able to win some of the most significant tournaments, I was presented with great trophies. These trophies represent special memories, both on and off the court—each one has a story to tell. Here I am holding a mini Davis Cup replica; a world championship winners coin from 1973; a gold medal from an exhibition tour of Saudi Arabia; a silver plate commemorating USC singles and doubles championships; and the U.S. Open singles trophy.

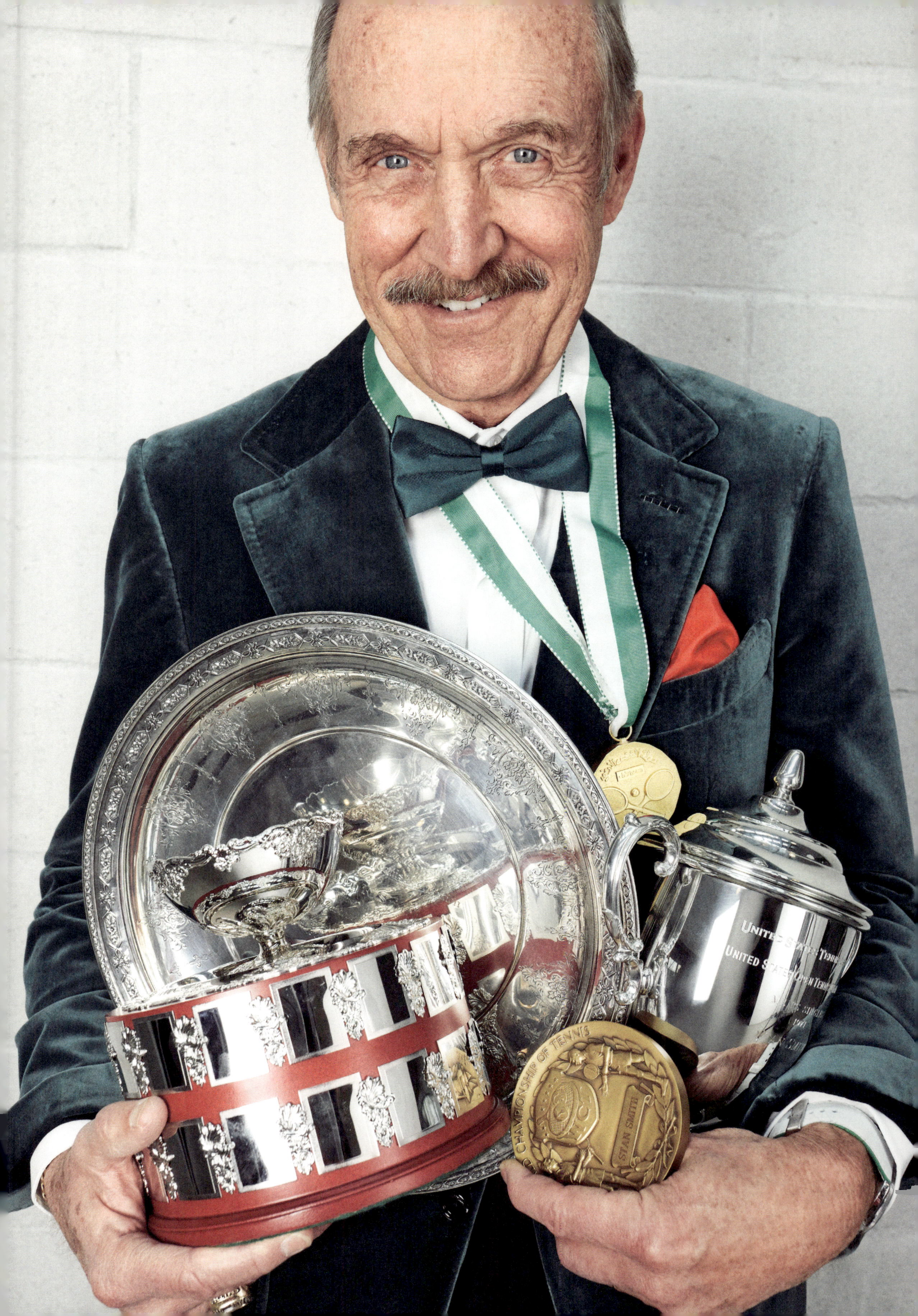
CHAMPIONSHIP OF TENNIS
STAN SMITH

2010:

Guest of Honor

My wife Margie and I have spent decades traveling the world together going from one tennis event to the next. We are regularly invited to all major tennis events and remain part of the global tennis community at large. From luxury suites to the Wimbledon Royal Box, we have had great seats next to celebrities and royalty. Margie kept her various "player's guest" credentials documenting our worldwide odyssey. She is displaying them while standing on real grass in her powerful serving position.

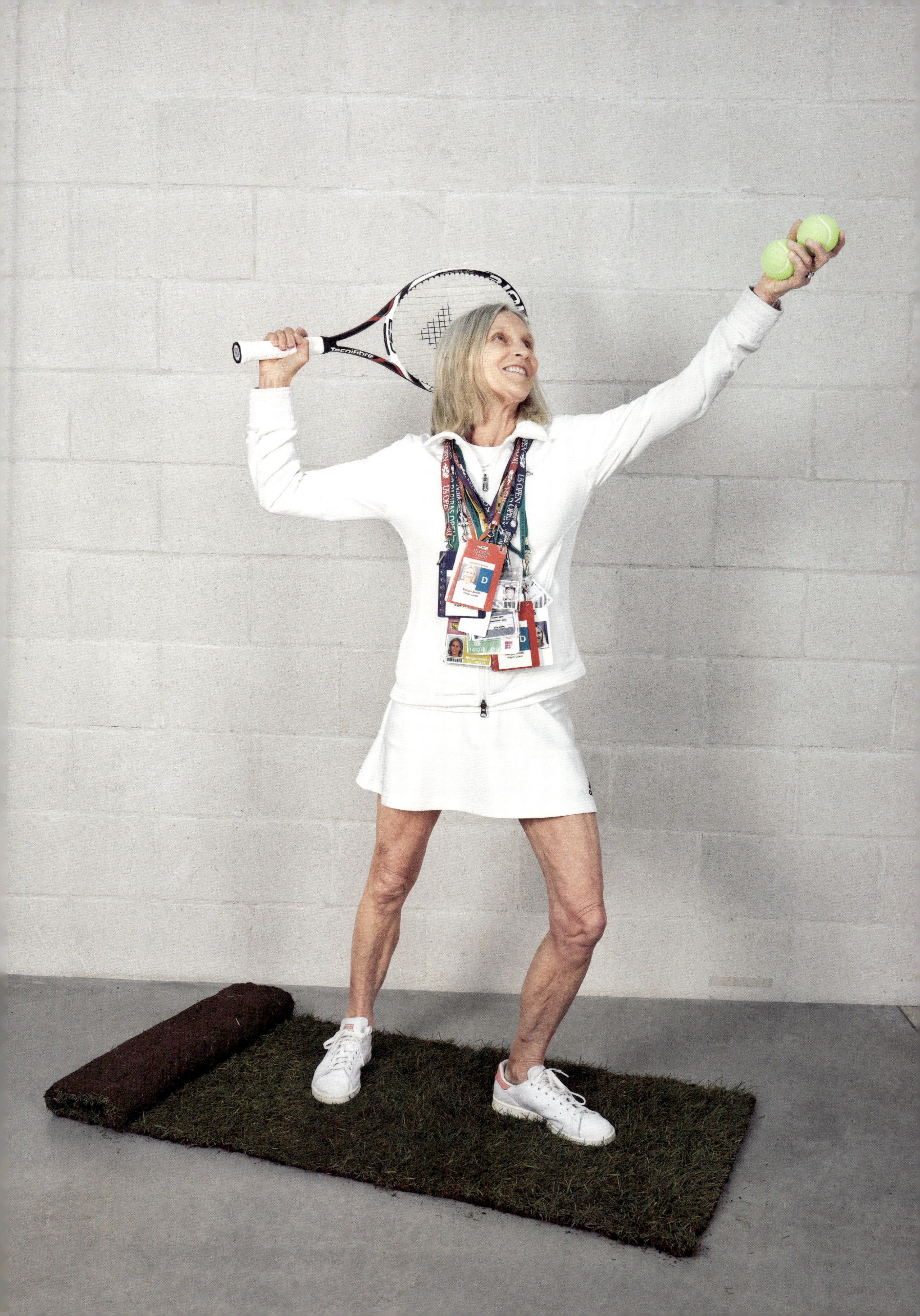

2014:

Sneakerhead's Dream

These are some of my favorite Stan Smith shoes, some that I designed and others that are a limited edition. I guess that I have become somewhat of a modern sneakerhead since my closet is full of both everyday and rare shoes that all happen to be Stan Smiths. I am surrounded by a colorful array of Stans showing the breadth of my iconic shoes. I am holding my prized custom Stan Smith clogs given to me in Amsterdam during the 2014 shoe relaunch campaign.

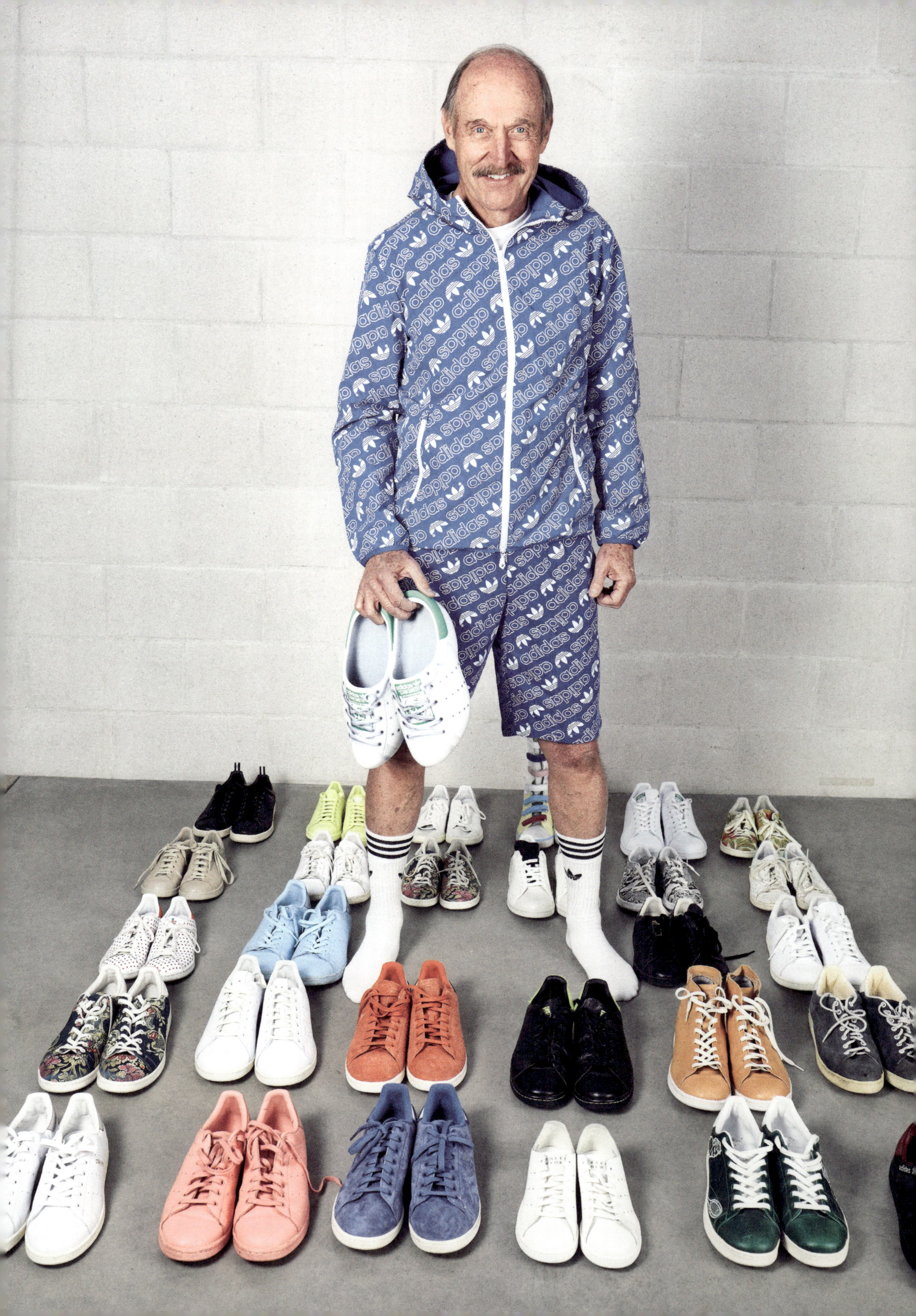
adidas

2018:

The Art of Stan

My shoe and its history of collaboration has inspired artists all over the world to create work both on the shoes and of the shoe itself, further enhancing its iconic status. I have seen exhibits in Melbourne, London, and New York.
In this image I am wearing super-sized ceramic shoes created by a young artist, Didi Rojas, whose obsession with the Stan Smith shoes, and sculptures, led her to create a piece of art which is quite magnificent.

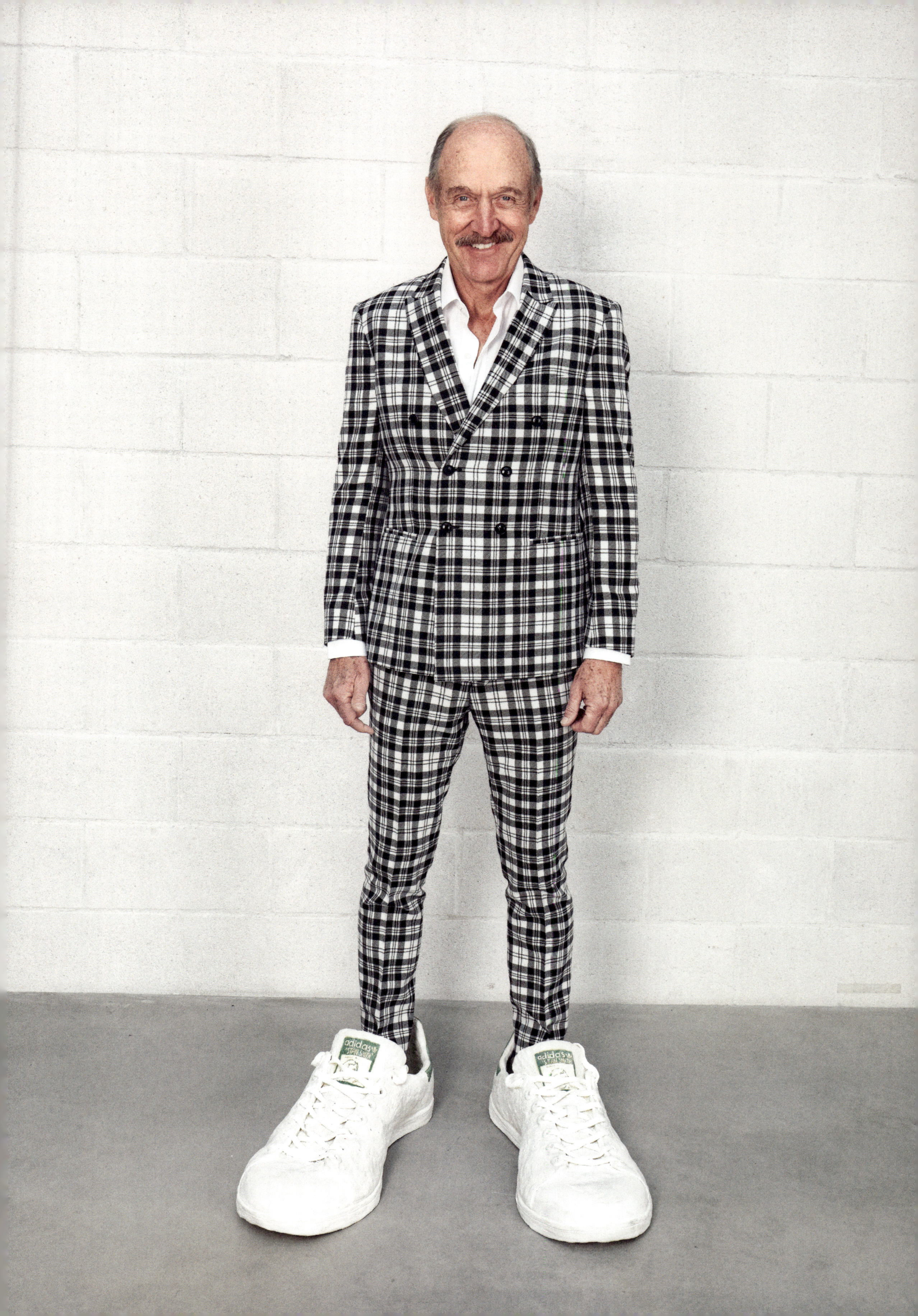
adidas
"STAN SMITH"
adidas
"STAN SMITH"

Some People Think I'm a Shoe!

Identity Crisis. A Shoe—Really?

Stan Smith

SOME PEOPLE THINK I'M A SHOE!

Acknowledgments

I would like to acknowledge adidas for believing in the vision, Rizzoli for coordinating the project, the team at Johannes Leonardo for their creative genius, my wife, Margie, for her support every step along the way, and Donald Dell for helping make this book happen. The shoe has been a special part of my life. – Stan Smith

Credits

Edited by:
Stan Smith, Richard Evans, Ferdinando Verderi, Maclean Jackson

Editorial, Creative and Design Direction by:
Ferdinando Verderi

Project Director: Sam McCallum

Art Director: Sylvia Gruber

Creative: Maclean Jackson, Mica Gallino

Project Manager: Tiff Liu

Producer: Adam Gong

Creative, Design, Production, Project Management team at Johannes Leonardo: Liz Moser, Alesa Blanchard Nelson, Alex Olivo, Maria Perez, Camilla Scales, Helena Martel Seward, Annie Sterenberg, Maddie Tiedrich

Thank you

Relentless support at adidas A.G: Dina Anani, Gary Aspden, Arnaud Biscay, Olivier Bourgis, Silvia Calligher, Terrell Clark, Rachel Ferrell, Annie Firth, Kerry Fisher, Luceny Fofana, Nic Galway, Paul Gaudio, Martin Gebhardt, Martin Herde, Arthur Hoeld, Kyle Irvin, Scott Johnston, Markus Kaiser, Masatoshi Kase, Paul Meany, Aline Mecke, Ashleigh Mellor, Alegra O'Hare, Christin Ott, Maura Pezzotta, Jenny Pham, Gabriel Schauf, Moritz Scherr, Ludovic Schuler, Torben Schumacher, Shinsuke Seta, Brianna Shimada, Andrea Swick, Alexander Unger, Alexandra Weiland, Jon Wexler, Christopher Wheat, Christian Wirth

And to: Charles Miers, Anthony Petrillose, Maria Pia Gramaglia, and Gisela Aguilar at Rizzoli International Publications

Special thanks to: Jason Coles, Juergen Teller, and Pharrell Williams for their exceptional contributions

And thank you to all the contributors to this book:
Junichi Abe, Yosuke Aizawa, Giovanni Alpi, Vijay Amritraj, Philip Andelman, Sarah Andelman, Daniel Arnold, Jeanne Moutoussamy-Ashe, Gary Aspden, Hailey Baldwin, Shane Battier, James Bond, Mac Cato, Jason Coles, Petra Collins, Sofia Coppola, Martina Cortese, Anthony Cotsifas, Donald Dell, Dippin' Sauce, Stefan Edberg, Pierre Elma, Allen Fox, Shigeki Fujishiro, Nic Galway, Paul Gaudio, Pooneh Ghoddoosi, Glenjamin, Jefferson Hack, Martin Herde, Masaaki Homma, Carlotta Ibba, Chris Jack, Sacha Jenkins, Poppy Kain, Craig Kallman, Tom Kemeny, Karlie Kloss, Adriana Mariella, Mark Mathabane, Carlos Mustienes, Martina Navratilova, Gary Niebur, Tsuyoshi Nimura, Yikiko Ode, Péle, J. Wayne Richmond, Didi Rojas, Weng San Lo, Jorge Santos, Jeremy Scott, Elizabeth Semmelhack, Olivia Silva, Raf Simons, Juergen Teller, Tei Towa, Karen Van Godtsenhoven, David Villa, Virginia Wade, Qiang Wenwen, Jon Wexler, Bill White, Pharrell Williams, Hideaki Yoshihara

First published in the United States of America in 2018 by
Rizzoli International Publications Inc.
300 Park Avenue South
New York, NY 10010
www.rizzoliusa.com

© 2018 Stan Smith

All rights reserved. No part of this publication may be reproduced, stored in retrieval systems, or transmitted in any form or by any means, electronic, mechanical, photocopying, recording, or otherwise, without the prior consent by the publishers.

Distributed in the U.S. trade by Random House, New York.

Publisher: Charles Miers
Associate Publisher: Anthony Petrillose
Editorial Assistance: Gisela Aguilar
Design Coordination: Kayleigh Jankowski
Production: Maria Pia Gramaglia
Copy Editors: Victorine Lamothe, Cindy Trickel

Printed in Italy

ISBN: 978-0-8478-6274-0
Library of Congress Control Number: 2018940295

2018 2019 2020 2021 / 10 9 8 7 6 5 4 3 2 1

Photography Credits

© Anthony Cotsifas, pages 56-57, 72, 82, 86-87 (bottom), 88 (right), 89 (top), 92-93, 105, 147, 156, 162, 181, 189, 206, 208, 209 (top and middle), 270, 272, 275, 281, 288, 297
© AP Images, pages 73, 271
© Christian McDonald, courtesy adidas, pages 8, 11
© Daniel Arnold, pages 70-71, 140-141, 246-247
© Daniel Riera, courtesy adidas, page 219
© Daily News, courtesy Stan Smith Archive, page 26
© David M. Spindel 1980, page 38
© Ed Fernberger, courtesy Stan Smith Archive, page 13
© Getty, pages 27, 64, 94-97, 99, 143, 182, 191, 196 (top)-197, 209 (bottom), 227-228, 231, 238, 254-255, 261, 273
© Howard Wechsler, page 106
© Jeanne Moutoussamy-Ashe, page 165
© Juergen Teller, pages 301, 303, 305, 307, 308-309, 311, 312-313, 315, 317, 319, 321, 323, 325, 327, 329
© Joao Canziani/August, pages 32-33, 132
© Marc Cato, courtesy Stan Smith Archive, page 275
© Petra Collins, page 245
© Ricky Powell, page 265
© Rineke Dijkstra, page 223
© Sarah Piantadosi, page 249
© Snowdon/Trunk Archive, page 36
© Stephen Vaughan, page 59
© Tennis, courtesy Stan Smith Archive, page 18
© Tennis U.S.A., courtesy Stan Smith Archive, page 19
© Tom Fey, page 188
© World Tennis, courtesy Stan Smith Archive, page 18, 170
courtesy adidas Archive, pages 35, 37-38, 41, 42, 43, 58, 60-61, 69, 76, 107, 131, 192, 213, 234
courtesy adidas Archive / studio Waldeck, pages 24-25, 40, 43, 44, 46-48, 62, 66-67, 74, 77-80, 84, 100, 102-103, 108, 118-120, 124-125, 128, 134-138, 144, 148, 154-155, 158, 166, 168-169, 176, 179, 183-186, 194, 200-201 (bottom), 202, 210, 212, 214-216, 220-222, 224-225, 232, 236-237, 242, 252, 257-258, 263, 266, 268, 278, 283-284, 286-287, 290-292

courtesy adidas Archive / Uli Kowatsch, page 23
courtesy Chris Jack, page 161
courtesy Craig Kallman, page 276
courtesy Didi Rojas, pages 90-91
courtesy of Dippin Sauce, photograph by David Filiberti, cover
courtesy Giovanni Alpi, page 241
courtesy James Bond, page 282
courtesy of JJMarshall Associates, photograph by Lacey, page 199
courtesy of Johannes Leonardo, photograph by Sylvia Gruber, page 235, photograph by Gonzalo Hergueta, pages 200-201 (top)
courtesy Mark Mathabane, page 114
courtesy of Princeton Alumni Weekly, page 104
courtesy Stan Smith Archive, pages 14-17, 20-22, 28-31, 50-57, 83, 86-89, 99, 110, 112-113, 116-117, 122, 127, 145, 150-153, 157, 163-164, 170-173, 175, 178, 190, 193, 196 (bottom), 205, 207, 239, 244, 250-251, 269, 280, 289, 294-296
courtesy Yosuke Aizawa, page 256

The photographs of Stan and Margie Smith by Juergen Teller were styled by Poppy Kain.

\#STANSMITHFOREVER

This book was inspired by all the stories I have heard, experienced, and seen over the years as I traveled the world. These are everyday stories that tell how the shoe became part of peoples lives, brought people together, created traditions, and witnessed memorable moments.

This book includes some of the stories. I would like to compile other narratives and testimonies from people in one place, which we will call #STANSMITHFOREVER. I would love to hear yours!

Stan